C-710 CAREER EXAMINATION SERIES

This is your
PASSBOOK for...

Senior Court Officer

Test Preparation Study Guide
Questions & Answers

NATIONAL LEARNING CORPORATION®

COPYRIGHT NOTICE

This book is SOLELY intended for, is sold ONLY to, and its use is RESTRICTED to individual, bona fide applicants or candidates who qualify by virtue of having seriously filed applications for appropriate license, certificate, professional and/or promotional advancement, higher school matriculation, scholarship, or other legitimate requirements of education and/or governmental authorities.

This book is NOT intended for use, class instruction, tutoring, training, duplication, copying, reprinting, excerption, or adaptation, etc., by:

1) Other publishers
2) Proprietors and/or Instructors of "Coaching" and/or Preparatory Courses
3) Personnel and/or Training Divisions of commercial, industrial, and governmental organizations
4) Schools, colleges, or universities and/or their departments and staffs, including teachers and other personnel
5) Testing Agencies or Bureaus
6) Study groups which seek by the purchase of a single volume to copy and/or duplicate and/or adapt this material for use by the group as a whole without having purchased individual volumes for each of the members of the group
7) Et al.

Such persons would be in violation of appropriate Federal and State statutes.

PROVISION OF LICENSING AGREEMENTS – Recognized educational, commercial, industrial, and governmental institutions and organizations, and others legitimately engaged in educational pursuits, including training, testing, and measurement activities, may address request for a licensing agreement to the copyright owners, who will determine whether, and under what conditions, including fees and charges, the materials in this book may be used them. In other words, a licensing facility exists for the legitimate use of the material in this book on other than an individual basis. However, it is asseverated and affirmed here that the material in this book CANNOT be used without the receipt of the express permission of such a licensing agreement from the Publishers. Inquiries re licensing should be addressed to the company, attention rights and permissions department.

All rights reserved, including the right of reproduction in whole or in part, in any form or by any means, electronic or mechanical, including photocopying, recording, or by any information storage and retrieval system, without permission in writing from the Publisher.

Copyright © 2025 by
National Learning Corporation

212 Michael Drive, Syosset, NY 11791
(516) 921-8888 • www.passbooks.com
E-mail: info@passbooks.com

PASSBOOK® SERIES

THE *PASSBOOK® SERIES* has been created to prepare applicants and candidates for the ultimate academic battlefield – the examination room.

At some time in our lives, each and every one of us may be required to take an examination – for validation, matriculation, admission, qualification, registration, certification, or licensure.

Based on the assumption that every applicant or candidate has met the basic formal educational standards, has taken the required number of courses, and read the necessary texts, the *PASSBOOK® SERIES* furnishes the one special preparation which may assure passing with confidence, instead of failing with insecurity. Examination questions – together with answers – are furnished as the basic vehicle for study so that the mysteries of the examination and its compounding difficulties may be eliminated or diminished by a sure method.

This book is meant to help you pass your examination provided that you qualify and are serious in your objective.

The entire field is reviewed through the huge store of content information which is succinctly presented through a provocative and challenging approach – the question-and-answer method.

A climate of success is established by furnishing the correct answers at the end of each test.

You soon learn to recognize types of questions, forms of questions, and patterns of questioning. You may even begin to anticipate expected outcomes.

You perceive that many questions are repeated or adapted so that you can gain acute insights, which may enable you to score many sure points.

You learn how to confront new questions, or types of questions, and to attack them confidently and work out the correct answers.

You note objectives and emphases, and recognize pitfalls and dangers, so that you may make positive educational adjustments.

Moreover, you are kept fully informed in relation to new concepts, methods, practices, and directions in the field.

You discover that you are actually taking the examination all the time: you are preparing for the examination by "taking" an examination, not by reading extraneous and/or supererogatory textbooks.

In short, this PASSBOOK®, used directedly, should be an important factor in helping you to pass your test.

SENIOR COURT OFFICER

DESCRIPTION OF DUTIES
Senior Court Officers are responsible for maintaining order and providing security in court buildings and courtrooms. They work under the direct supervision of security supervisors and court clerks. Senior Court Officers are peace officers, required to wear uniforms, and may be authorized to carry firearms. Senior Court Officers execute warrants and make arrests and may coordinate the activities of other court security personnel.

Examples of typical tasks: Provides security by standing in the courtroom and patrolling the courthouse; guards felons and persons accused of felonies, and may guard individuals accused of lesser crimes while they are in the courtroom and escorts them to and from detention pens; physically restrains unruly individuals: uses established search procedures to assure that no weapons or electronic or photographic equipment are brought into the courtroom; escorts judges, juries, witnesses and prisoners to and from the courtroom; escorts, guards, and delivers material to sequestered juries; provides general information to visitors on court premises; checks to insure that all necessary documents are available prior to court sessions; displays and safeguards exhibits in the courtroom; provides assistance in emergency situations; maintains and updates court records and prepares incident reports; distributes and posts appropriate documents and court records; arrests individuals according to established procedures.

WRITTEN EXAMINATION
The written examination will be multiple-choice and will assess a candidate's ability to:
    I. Read, Understand, and Interpret Written Material
        Candidates will be presented with brief reading selections followed by questions relating to the selections. All of the information required to answer the questions will be provided in the selections: candidates will not be required to have any special knowledge relating to the content area covered in the selections.
    II. Remember Facts and Information
        Candidates will be provided with a description of an event or incident. After a brief period of time to review and study the description, the description will be removed from the candidates. Candidates will later be asked questions about the facts involved in the event or incident without access to the description.
    III. Apply Facts and Information to Given Situations
        Candidates will be provided with facts and information and will be asked questions that require the application of these facts and information to specific actions that should be taken in a given situation.
    IV. Peace Officer Knowledge
        Candidates will be presented with questions that are designed to test knowledge of the Criminal Procedure Law and the Penal Law, including, but not limited to, the law of arrest, search procedures use of firearms, and the use of physical force.

HOW TO TAKE A TEST

I. YOU MUST PASS AN EXAMINATION

A. *WHAT EVERY CANDIDATE SHOULD KNOW*

Examination applicants often ask us for help in preparing for the written test. What can I study in advance? What kinds of questions will be asked? How will the test be given? How will the papers be graded?

As an applicant for a civil service examination, you may be wondering about some of these things. Our purpose here is to suggest effective methods of advance study and to describe civil service examinations.

Your chances for success on this examination can be increased if you know how to prepare. Those "pre-examination jitters" can be reduced if you know what to expect. You can even experience an adventure in good citizenship if you know why civil service exams are given.

B. *WHY ARE CIVIL SERVICE EXAMINATIONS GIVEN?*

Civil service examinations are important to you in two ways. As a citizen, you want public jobs filled by employees who know how to do their work. As a job seeker, you want a fair chance to compete for that job on an equal footing with other candidates. The best-known means of accomplishing this two-fold goal is the competitive examination.

Exams are widely publicized throughout the nation. They may be administered for jobs in federal, state, city, municipal, town or village governments or agencies.

Any citizen may apply, with some limitations, such as the age or residence of applicants. Your experience and education may be reviewed to see whether you meet the requirements for the particular examination. When these requirements exist, they are reasonable and applied consistently to all applicants. Thus, a competitive examination may cause you some uneasiness now, but it is your privilege and safeguard.

C. *HOW ARE CIVIL SERVICE EXAMS DEVELOPED?*

Examinations are carefully written by trained technicians who are specialists in the field known as "psychological measurement," in consultation with recognized authorities in the field of work that the test will cover. These experts recommend the subject matter areas or skills to be tested; only those knowledges or skills important to your success on the job are included. The most reliable books and source materials available are used as references. Together, the experts and technicians judge the difficulty level of the questions.

Test technicians know how to phrase questions so that the problem is clearly stated. Their ethics do not permit "trick" or "catch" questions. Questions may have been tried out on sample groups, or subjected to statistical analysis, to determine their usefulness.

Written tests are often used in combination with performance tests, ratings of training and experience, and oral interviews. All of these measures combine to form the best-known means of finding the right person for the right job.

II. HOW TO PASS THE WRITTEN TEST

A. NATURE OF THE EXAMINATION

To prepare intelligently for civil service examinations, you should know how they differ from school examinations you have taken. In school you were assigned certain definite pages to read or subjects to cover. The examination questions were quite detailed and usually emphasized memory. Civil service exams, on the other hand, try to discover your present ability to perform the duties of a position, plus your potentiality to learn these duties. In other words, a civil service exam attempts to predict how successful you will be. Questions cover such a broad area that they cannot be as minute and detailed as school exam questions.

In the public service similar kinds of work, or positions, are grouped together in one "class." This process is known as *position-classification*. All the positions in a class are paid according to the salary range for that class. One class title covers all of these positions, and they are all tested by the same examination.

B. FOUR BASIC STEPS

1) Study the announcement

How, then, can you know what subjects to study? Our best answer is: "Learn as much as possible about the class of positions for which you've applied." The exam will test the knowledge, skills and abilities needed to do the work.

Your most valuable source of information about the position you want is the official exam announcement. This announcement lists the training and experience qualifications. Check these standards and apply only if you come reasonably close to meeting them.

The brief description of the position in the examination announcement offers some clues to the subjects which will be tested. Think about the job itself. Review the duties in your mind. Can you perform them, or are there some in which you are rusty? Fill in the blank spots in your preparation.

Many jurisdictions preview the written test in the exam announcement by including a section called "Knowledge and Abilities Required," "Scope of the Examination," or some similar heading. Here you will find out specifically what fields will be tested.

2) Review your own background

Once you learn in general what the position is all about, and what you need to know to do the work, ask yourself which subjects you already know fairly well and which need improvement. You may wonder whether to concentrate on improving your strong areas or on building some background in your fields of weakness. When the announcement has specified "some knowledge" or "considerable knowledge," or has used adjectives like "beginning principles of..." or "advanced ... methods," you can get a clue as to the number and difficulty of questions to be asked in any given field. More questions, and hence broader coverage, would be included for those subjects which are more important in the work. Now weigh your strengths and weaknesses against the job requirements and prepare accordingly.

3) Determine the level of the position

Another way to tell how intensively you should prepare is to understand the level of the job for which you are applying. Is it the entering level? In other words, is this the position in which beginners in a field of work are hired? Or is it an intermediate or advanced level? Sometimes this is indicated by such words as "Junior" or "Senior" in the class title. Other jurisdictions use Roman numerals to designate the level – Clerk I, Clerk II, for example. The word "Supervisor" sometimes appears in the title. If the level is not indicated by the title, check the description of duties. Will you be working under very close supervision, or will you have responsibility for independent decisions in this work?

4) Choose appropriate study materials

Now that you know the subjects to be examined and the relative amount of each subject to be covered, you can choose suitable study materials. For beginning level jobs, or even advanced ones, if you have a pronounced weakness in some aspect of your training, read a modern, standard textbook in that field. Be sure it is up to date and has general coverage. Such books are normally available at your library, and the librarian will be glad to help you locate one. For entry-level positions, questions of appropriate difficulty are chosen – neither highly advanced questions, nor those too simple. Such questions require careful thought but not advanced training.

If the position for which you are applying is technical or advanced, you will read more advanced, specialized material. If you are already familiar with the basic principles of your field, elementary textbooks would waste your time. Concentrate on advanced textbooks and technical periodicals. Think through the concepts and review difficult problems in your field.

These are all general sources. You can get more ideas on your own initiative, following these leads. For example, training manuals and publications of the government agency which employs workers in your field can be useful, particularly for technical and professional positions. A letter or visit to the government department involved may result in more specific study suggestions, and certainly will provide you with a more definite idea of the exact nature of the position you are seeking.

III. KINDS OF TESTS

Tests are used for purposes other than measuring knowledge and ability to perform specified duties. For some positions, it is equally important to test ability to make adjustments to new situations or to profit from training. In others, basic mental abilities not dependent on information are essential. Questions which test these things may not appear as pertinent to the duties of the position as those which test for knowledge and information. Yet they are often highly important parts of a fair examination. For very general questions, it is almost impossible to help you direct your study efforts. What we can do is to point out some of the more common of these general abilities needed in public service positions and describe some typical questions.

1) General information

Broad, general information has been found useful for predicting job success in some kinds of work. This is tested in a variety of ways, from vocabulary lists to questions about current events. Basic background in some field of work, such as sociology or economics, may be sampled in a group of questions. Often these are principles which have become familiar to most persons through exposure rather than through formal training. It is difficult to advise you how to study for these questions; being alert to the world around you is our best suggestion.

2) Verbal ability

An example of an ability needed in many positions is verbal or language ability. Verbal ability is, in brief, the ability to use and understand words. Vocabulary and grammar tests are typical measures of this ability. Reading comprehension or paragraph interpretation questions are common in many kinds of civil service tests. You are given a paragraph of written material and asked to find its central meaning.

3) Numerical ability

Number skills can be tested by the familiar arithmetic problem, by checking paired lists of numbers to see which are alike and which are different, or by interpreting charts and graphs. In the latter test, a graph may be printed in the test booklet which you are asked to use as the basis for answering questions.

4) Observation

A popular test for law-enforcement positions is the observation test. A picture is shown to you for several minutes, then taken away. Questions about the picture test your ability to observe both details and larger elements.

5) Following directions

In many positions in the public service, the employee must be able to carry out written instructions dependably and accurately. You may be given a chart with several columns, each column listing a variety of information. The questions require you to carry out directions involving the information given in the chart.

6) Skills and aptitudes

Performance tests effectively measure some manual skills and aptitudes. When the skill is one in which you are trained, such as typing or shorthand, you can practice. These tests are often very much like those given in business school or high school courses. For many of the other skills and aptitudes, however, no short-time preparation can be made. Skills and abilities natural to you or that you have developed throughout your lifetime are being tested.

Many of the general questions just described provide all the data needed to answer the questions and ask you to use your reasoning ability to find the answers. Your best preparation for these tests, as well as for tests of facts and ideas, is to be at your physical and mental best. You, no doubt, have your own methods of getting into an exam-taking mood and keeping "in shape." The next section lists some ideas on this subject.

IV. KINDS OF QUESTIONS

Only rarely is the "essay" question, which you answer in narrative form, used in civil service tests. Civil service tests are usually of the short-answer type. Full instructions for answering these questions will be given to you at the examination. But in case this is your first experience with short-answer questions and separate answer sheets, here is what you need to know:

1) Multiple-choice Questions

Most popular of the short-answer questions is the "multiple choice" or "best answer" question. It can be used, for example, to test for factual knowledge, ability to solve problems or judgment in meeting situations found at work.

A multiple-choice question is normally one of three types—
- It can begin with an incomplete statement followed by several possible endings. You are to find the one ending which *best* completes the statement, although some of the others may not be entirely wrong.
- It can also be a complete statement in the form of a question which is answered by choosing one of the statements listed.

- It can be in the form of a problem – again you select the best answer.

Here is an example of a multiple-choice question with a discussion which should give you some clues as to the method for choosing the right answer:

When an employee has a complaint about his assignment, the action which will *best* help him overcome his difficulty is to
  A. discuss his difficulty with his coworkers
  B. take the problem to the head of the organization
  C. take the problem to the person who gave him the assignment
  D. say nothing to anyone about his complaint

In answering this question, you should study each of the choices to find which is best. Consider choice "A" – Certainly an employee may discuss his complaint with fellow employees, but no change or improvement can result, and the complaint remains unresolved. Choice "B" is a poor choice since the head of the organization probably does not know what assignment you have been given, and taking your problem to him is known as "going over the head" of the supervisor. The supervisor, or person who made the assignment, is the person who can clarify it or correct any injustice. Choice "C" is, therefore, correct. To say nothing, as in choice "D," is unwise. Supervisors have and interest in knowing the problems employees are facing, and the employee is seeking a solution to his problem.

2) True/False Questions

The "true/false" or "right/wrong" form of question is sometimes used. Here a complete statement is given. Your job is to decide whether the statement is right or wrong.

SAMPLE: A roaming cell-phone call to a nearby city costs less than a non-roaming call to a distant city.

This statement is wrong, or false, since roaming calls are more expensive.

This is not a complete list of all possible question forms, although most of the others are variations of these common types. You will always get complete directions for answering questions. Be sure you understand *how* to mark your answers – ask questions until you do.

V. RECORDING YOUR ANSWERS

Computer terminals are used more and more today for many different kinds of exams.

For an examination with very few applicants, you may be told to record your answers in the test booklet itself. Separate answer sheets are much more common. If this separate answer sheet is to be scored by machine – and this is often the case – it is highly important that you mark your answers correctly in order to get credit.

An electronic scoring machine is often used in civil service offices because of the speed with which papers can be scored. Machine-scored answer sheets must be marked with a pencil, which will be given to you. This pencil has a high graphite content which responds to the electronic scoring machine. As a matter of fact, stray dots may register as answers, so do not let your pencil rest on the answer sheet while you are pondering the correct answer. Also, if your pencil lead breaks or is otherwise defective, ask for another.

Since the answer sheet will be dropped in a slot in the scoring machine, be careful not to bend the corners or get the paper crumpled.

The answer sheet normally has five vertical columns of numbers, with 30 numbers to a column. These numbers correspond to the question numbers in your test booklet. After each number, going across the page are four or five pairs of dotted lines. These short dotted lines have small letters or numbers above them. The first two pairs may also have a "T" or "F" above the letters. This indicates that the first two pairs only are to be used if the questions are of the true-false type. If the questions are multiple choice, disregard the "T" and "F" and pay attention only to the small letters or numbers.

Answer your questions in the manner of the sample that follows:

32. The largest city in the United States is
    A. Washington, D.C.
    B. New York City
    C. Chicago
    D. Detroit
    E. San Francisco

1) Choose the answer you think is best. (New York City is the largest, so "B" is correct.)
2) Find the row of dotted lines numbered the same as the question you are answering. (Find row number 32)
3) Find the pair of dotted lines corresponding to the answer. (Find the pair of lines under the mark "B.")
4) Make a solid black mark between the dotted lines.

VI. BEFORE THE TEST

Common sense will help you find procedures to follow to get ready for an examination. Too many of us, however, overlook these sensible measures. Indeed, nervousness and fatigue have been found to be the most serious reasons why applicants fail to do their best on civil service tests. Here is a list of reminders:

- Begin your preparation early – Don't wait until the last minute to go scurrying around for books and materials or to find out what the position is all about.
- Prepare continuously – An hour a night for a week is better than an all-night cram session. This has been definitely established. What is more, a night a week for a month will return better dividends than crowding your study into a shorter period of time.
- Locate the place of the exam – You have been sent a notice telling you when and where to report for the examination. If the location is in a different town or otherwise unfamiliar to you, it would be well to inquire the best route and learn something about the building.
- Relax the night before the test – Allow your mind to rest. Do not study at all that night. Plan some mild recreation or diversion; then go to bed early and get a good night's sleep.
- Get up early enough to make a leisurely trip to the place for the test – This way unforeseen events, traffic snarls, unfamiliar buildings, etc. will not upset you.
- Dress comfortably – A written test is not a fashion show. You will be known by number and not by name, so wear something comfortable.

- Leave excess paraphernalia at home – Shopping bags and odd bundles will get in your way. You need bring only the items mentioned in the official notice you received; usually everything you need is provided. Do not bring reference books to the exam. They will only confuse those last minutes and be taken away from you when in the test room.
- Arrive somewhat ahead of time – If because of transportation schedules you must get there very early, bring a newspaper or magazine to take your mind off yourself while waiting.
- Locate the examination room – When you have found the proper room, you will be directed to the seat or part of the room where you will sit. Sometimes you are given a sheet of instructions to read while you are waiting. Do not fill out any forms until you are told to do so; just read them and be prepared.
- Relax and prepare to listen to the instructions
- If you have any physical problem that may keep you from doing your best, be sure to tell the test administrator. If you are sick or in poor health, you really cannot do your best on the exam. You can come back and take the test some other time.

VII. AT THE TEST

The day of the test is here and you have the test booklet in your hand. The temptation to get going is very strong. Caution! There is more to success than knowing the right answers. You must know how to identify your papers and understand variations in the type of short-answer question used in this particular examination. Follow these suggestions for maximum results from your efforts:

1) Cooperate with the monitor

The test administrator has a duty to create a situation in which you can be as much at ease as possible. He will give instructions, tell you when to begin, check to see that you are marking your answer sheet correctly, and so on. He is not there to guard you, although he will see that your competitors do not take unfair advantage. He wants to help you do your best.

2) Listen to all instructions

Don't jump the gun! Wait until you understand all directions. In most civil service tests you get more time than you need to answer the questions. So don't be in a hurry. Read each word of instructions until you clearly understand the meaning. Study the examples, listen to all announcements and follow directions. Ask questions if you do not understand what to do.

3) Identify your papers

Civil service exams are usually identified by number only. You will be assigned a number; you must not put your name on your test papers. Be sure to copy your number correctly. Since more than one exam may be given, copy your exact examination title.

4) Plan your time

Unless you are told that a test is a "speed" or "rate of work" test, speed itself is usually not important. Time enough to answer all the questions will be provided, but this does not mean that you have all day. An overall time limit has been set. Divide the total time (in minutes) by the number of questions to determine the approximate time you have for each question.

5) Do not linger over difficult questions

If you come across a difficult question, mark it with a paper clip (useful to have along) and come back to it when you have been through the booklet. One caution if you do this – be sure to skip a number on your answer sheet as well. Check often to be sure that you have not lost your place and that you are marking in the row numbered the same as the question you are answering.

6) Read the questions

Be sure you know what the question asks! Many capable people are unsuccessful because they failed to *read* the questions correctly.

7) Answer all questions

Unless you have been instructed that a penalty will be deducted for incorrect answers, it is better to guess than to omit a question.

8) Speed tests

It is often better NOT to guess on speed tests. It has been found that on timed tests people are tempted to spend the last few seconds before time is called in marking answers at random – without even reading them – in the hope of picking up a few extra points. To discourage this practice, the instructions may warn you that your score will be "corrected" for guessing. That is, a penalty will be applied. The incorrect answers will be deducted from the correct ones, or some other penalty formula will be used.

9) Review your answers

If you finish before time is called, go back to the questions you guessed or omitted to give them further thought. Review other answers if you have time.

10) Return your test materials

If you are ready to leave before others have finished or time is called, take ALL your materials to the monitor and leave quietly. Never take any test material with you. The monitor can discover whose papers are not complete, and taking a test booklet may be grounds for disqualification.

VIII. EXAMINATION TECHNIQUES

1) Read the general instructions carefully. These are usually printed on the first page of the exam booklet. As a rule, these instructions refer to the timing of the examination; the fact that you should not start work until the signal and must stop work at a signal, etc. If there are any *special* instructions, such as a choice of questions to be answered, make sure that you note this instruction carefully.

2) When you are ready to start work on the examination, that is as soon as the signal has been given, read the instructions to each question booklet, underline any key words or phrases, such as *least, best, outline, describe* and the like. In this way you will tend to answer as requested rather than discover on reviewing your paper that you *listed without describing*, that you selected the *worst* choice rather than the *best* choice, etc.

3) If the examination is of the objective or multiple-choice type – that is, each question will also give a series of possible answers: A, B, C or D, and you are called upon to select the best answer and write the letter next to that answer on your answer paper – it is advisable to start answering each question in turn. There may be anywhere from 50 to 100 such questions in the three or four hours allotted and you can see how much time would be taken if you read through all the questions before beginning to answer any. Furthermore, if you come across a question or group of questions which you know would be difficult to answer, it would undoubtedly affect your handling of all the other questions.

4) If the examination is of the essay type and contains but a few questions, it is a moot point as to whether you should read all the questions before starting to answer any one. Of course, if you are given a choice – say five out of seven and the like – then it is essential to read all the questions so you can eliminate the two that are most difficult. If, however, you are asked to answer all the questions, there may be danger in trying to answer the easiest one first because you may find that you will spend too much time on it. The best technique is to answer the first question, then proceed to the second, etc.

5) Time your answers. Before the exam begins, write down the time it started, then add the time allowed for the examination and write down the time it must be completed, then divide the time available somewhat as follows:
   - If 3-1/2 hours are allowed, that would be 210 minutes. If you have 80 objective-type questions, that would be an average of 2-1/2 minutes per question. Allow yourself no more than 2 minutes per question, or a total of 160 minutes, which will permit about 50 minutes to review.
   - If for the time allotment of 210 minutes there are 7 essay questions to answer, that would average about 30 minutes a question. Give yourself only 25 minutes per question so that you have about 35 minutes to review.

6) The most important instruction is to *read each question* and make sure you know what is wanted. The second most important instruction is to *time yourself properly* so that you answer every question. The third most important instruction is to *answer every question*. Guess if you have to but include something for each question. Remember that you will receive no credit for a blank and will probably receive some credit if you write something in answer to an essay question. If you guess a letter – say "B" for a multiple-choice question – you may have guessed right. If you leave a blank as an answer to a multiple-choice question, the examiners may respect your feelings but it will not add a point to your score. Some exams may penalize you for wrong answers, so in such cases *only*, you may not want to guess unless you have some basis for your answer.

7) Suggestions
   a. Objective-type questions
      1. Examine the question booklet for proper sequence of pages and questions
      2. Read all instructions carefully
      3. Skip any question which seems too difficult; return to it after all other questions have been answered
      4. Apportion your time properly; do not spend too much time on any single question or group of questions

5. Note and underline key words – *all, most, fewest, least, best, worst, same, opposite,* etc.
6. Pay particular attention to negatives
7. Note unusual option, e.g., unduly long, short, complex, different or similar in content to the body of the question
8. Observe the use of "hedging" words – *probably, may, most likely,* etc.
9. Make sure that your answer is put next to the same number as the question
10. Do not second-guess unless you have good reason to believe the second answer is definitely more correct
11. Cross out original answer if you decide another answer is more accurate; do not erase until you are ready to hand your paper in
12. Answer all questions; guess unless instructed otherwise
13. Leave time for review

b. Essay questions
   1. Read each question carefully
   2. Determine exactly what is wanted. Underline key words or phrases.
   3. Decide on outline or paragraph answer
   4. Include many different points and elements unless asked to develop any one or two points or elements
   5. Show impartiality by giving pros and cons unless directed to select one side only
   6. Make and write down any assumptions you find necessary to answer the questions
   7. Watch your English, grammar, punctuation and choice of words
   8. Time your answers; don't crowd material

8) Answering the essay question

Most essay questions can be answered by framing the specific response around several key words or ideas. Here are a few such key words or ideas:

M's: manpower, materials, methods, money, management
P's: purpose, program, policy, plan, procedure, practice, problems, pitfalls, personnel, public relations

   a. Six basic steps in handling problems:
      1. Preliminary plan and background development
      2. Collect information, data and facts
      3. Analyze and interpret information, data and facts
      4. Analyze and develop solutions as well as make recommendations
      5. Prepare report and sell recommendations
      6. Install recommendations and follow up effectiveness

   b. Pitfalls to avoid
      1. *Taking things for granted* – A statement of the situation does not necessarily imply that each of the elements is necessarily true; for example, a complaint may be invalid and biased so that all that can be taken for granted is that a complaint has been registered

2. *Considering only one side of a situation* – Wherever possible, indicate several alternatives and then point out the reasons you selected the best one
3. *Failing to indicate follow up* – Whenever your answer indicates action on your part, make certain that you will take proper follow-up action to see how successful your recommendations, procedures or actions turn out to be
4. *Taking too long in answering any single question* – Remember to time your answers properly

IX. AFTER THE TEST

Scoring procedures differ in detail among civil service jurisdictions although the general principles are the same. Whether the papers are hand-scored or graded by machine we have described, they are nearly always graded by number. That is, the person who marks the paper knows only the number – never the name – of the applicant. Not until all the papers have been graded will they be matched with names. If other tests, such as training and experience or oral interview ratings have been given, scores will be combined. Different parts of the examination usually have different weights. For example, the written test might count 60 percent of the final grade, and a rating of training and experience 40 percent. In many jurisdictions, veterans will have a certain number of points added to their grades.

After the final grade has been determined, the names are placed in grade order and an eligible list is established. There are various methods for resolving ties between those who get the same final grade – probably the most common is to place first the name of the person whose application was received first. Job offers are made from the eligible list in the order the names appear on it. You will be notified of your grade and your rank as soon as all these computations have been made. This will be done as rapidly as possible.

People who are found to meet the requirements in the announcement are called "eligibles." Their names are put on a list of eligible candidates. An eligible's chances of getting a job depend on how high he stands on this list and how fast agencies are filling jobs from the list.

When a job is to be filled from a list of eligibles, the agency asks for the names of people on the list of eligibles for that job. When the civil service commission receives this request, it sends to the agency the names of the three people highest on this list. Or, if the job to be filled has specialized requirements, the office sends the agency the names of the top three persons who meet these requirements from the general list.

The appointing officer makes a choice from among the three people whose names were sent to him. If the selected person accepts the appointment, the names of the others are put back on the list to be considered for future openings.

That is the rule in hiring from all kinds of eligible lists, whether they are for typist, carpenter, chemist, or something else. For every vacancy, the appointing officer has his choice of any one of the top three eligibles on the list. This explains why the person whose name is on top of the list sometimes does not get an appointment when some of the persons lower on the list do. If the appointing officer chooses the second or third eligible, the No. 1 eligible does not get a job at once, but stays on the list until he is appointed or the list is terminated.

X. HOW TO PASS THE INTERVIEW TEST

The examination for which you applied requires an oral interview test. You have already taken the written test and you are now being called for the interview test – the final part of the formal examination.

You may think that it is not possible to prepare for an interview test and that there are no procedures to follow during an interview. Our purpose is to point out some things you can do in advance that will help you and some good rules to follow and pitfalls to avoid while you are being interviewed.

What is an interview supposed to test?

The written examination is designed to test the technical knowledge and competence of the candidate; the oral is designed to evaluate intangible qualities, not readily measured otherwise, and to establish a list showing the relative fitness of each candidate – as measured against his competitors – for the position sought. Scoring is not on the basis of "right" and "wrong," but on a sliding scale of values ranging from "not passable" to "outstanding." As a matter of fact, it is possible to achieve a relatively low score without a single "incorrect" answer because of evident weakness in the qualities being measured.

Occasionally, an examination may consist entirely of an oral test – either an individual or a group oral. In such cases, information is sought concerning the technical knowledges and abilities of the candidate, since there has been no written examination for this purpose. More commonly, however, an oral test is used to supplement a written examination.

Who conducts interviews?

The composition of oral boards varies among different jurisdictions. In nearly all, a representative of the personnel department serves as chairman. One of the members of the board may be a representative of the department in which the candidate would work. In some cases, "outside experts" are used, and, frequently, a businessman or some other representative of the general public is asked to serve. Labor and management or other special groups may be represented. The aim is to secure the services of experts in the appropriate field.

However the board is composed, it is a good idea (and not at all improper or unethical) to ascertain in advance of the interview who the members are and what groups they represent. When you are introduced to them, you will have some idea of their backgrounds and interests, and at least you will not stutter and stammer over their names.

What should be done before the interview?

While knowledge about the board members is useful and takes some of the surprise element out of the interview, there is other preparation which is more substantive. It *is* possible to prepare for an oral interview – in several ways:

1) Keep a copy of your application and review it carefully before the interview

This may be the only document before the oral board, and the starting point of the interview. Know what education and experience you have listed there, and the sequence and dates of all of it. Sometimes the board will ask you to review the highlights of your experience for them; you should not have to hem and haw doing it.

2) Study the class specification and the examination announcement

Usually, the oral board has one or both of these to guide them. The qualities, characteristics or knowledges required by the position sought are stated in these documents. They offer valuable clues as to the nature of the oral interview. For example, if the job involves supervisory responsibilities, the announcement will usually indicate that knowledge of modern supervisory methods and the qualifications of the candidate as a supervisor will be tested. If so, you can expect such questions, frequently in the form of a hypothetical situation which you are expected to solve. NEVER go into an oral without knowledge of the duties and responsibilities of the job you seek.

3) Think through each qualification required

Try to visualize the kind of questions you would ask if you were a board member. How well could you answer them? Try especially to appraise your own knowledge and background in each area, *measured against the job sought*, and identify any areas in which you are weak. Be critical and realistic – do not flatter yourself.

4) Do some general reading in areas in which you feel you may be weak

For example, if the job involves supervision and your past experience has NOT, some general reading in supervisory methods and practices, particularly in the field of human relations, might be useful. Do NOT study agency procedures or detailed manuals. The oral board will be testing your understanding and capacity, not your memory.

5) Get a good night's sleep and watch your general health and mental attitude

You will want a clear head at the interview. Take care of a cold or any other minor ailment, and of course, no hangovers.

What should be done on the day of the interview?

Now comes the day of the interview itself. Give yourself plenty of time to get there. Plan to arrive somewhat ahead of the scheduled time, particularly if your appointment is in the fore part of the day. If a previous candidate fails to appear, the board might be ready for you a bit early. By early afternoon an oral board is almost invariably behind schedule if there are many candidates, and you may have to wait. Take along a book or magazine to read, or your application to review, but leave any extraneous material in the waiting room when you go in for your interview. In any event, relax and compose yourself.

The matter of dress is important. The board is forming impressions about you – from your experience, your manners, your attitude, and your appearance. Give your personal appearance careful attention. Dress your best, but not your flashiest. Choose conservative, appropriate clothing, and be sure it is immaculate. This is a business interview, and your appearance should indicate that you regard it as such. Besides, being well groomed and properly dressed will help boost your confidence.

Sooner or later, someone will call your name and escort you into the interview room. *This is it.* From here on you are on your own. It is too late for any more preparation. But remember, you asked for this opportunity to prove your fitness, and you are here because your request was granted.

What happens when you go in?

The usual sequence of events will be as follows: The clerk (who is often the board stenographer) will introduce you to the chairman of the oral board, who will introduce you to the other members of the board. Acknowledge the introductions before you sit down. Do not be surprised if you find a microphone facing you or a stenotypist sitting by. Oral interviews are usually recorded in the event of an appeal or other review.

Usually the chairman of the board will open the interview by reviewing the highlights of your education and work experience from your application – primarily for the benefit of the other members of the board, as well as to get the material into the record. Do not interrupt or comment unless there is an error or significant misinterpretation; if that is the case, do not hesitate. But do not quibble about insignificant matters. Also, he will usually ask you some question about your education, experience or your present job – partly to get you to start talking and to establish the interviewing "rapport." He may start the actual questioning, or turn it over to one of the other members. Frequently, each member undertakes the questioning on a particular area, one in which he is perhaps most competent, so you can expect each member to participate in the examination. Because time is limited, you may also expect some rather abrupt switches in the direction the questioning takes, so do not be upset by it. Normally, a board member will not pursue a single line of questioning unless he discovers a particular strength or weakness.

After each member has participated, the chairman will usually ask whether any member has any further questions, then will ask you if you have anything you wish to add. Unless you are expecting this question, it may floor you. Worse, it may start you off on an extended, extemporaneous speech. The board is not usually seeking more information. The question is principally to offer you a last opportunity to present further qualifications or to indicate that you have nothing to add. So, if you feel that a significant qualification or characteristic has been overlooked, it is proper to point it out in a sentence or so. Do not compliment the board on the thoroughness of their examination – they have been sketchy, and you know it. If you wish, merely say, "No thank you, I have nothing further to add." This is a point where you can "talk yourself out" of a good impression or fail to present an important bit of information. Remember, *you close the interview yourself.*

The chairman will then say, "That is all, Mr. _____, thank you." Do not be startled; the interview is over, and quicker than you think. Thank him, gather your belongings and take your leave. Save your sigh of relief for the other side of the door.

How to put your best foot forward
Throughout this entire process, you may feel that the board individually and collectively is trying to pierce your defenses, seek out your hidden weaknesses and embarrass and confuse you. Actually, this is not true. They are obliged to make an appraisal of your qualifications for the job you are seeking, and they want to see you in your best light. Remember, they must interview all candidates and a non-cooperative candidate may become a failure in spite of their best efforts to bring out his qualifications. Here are 15 suggestions that will help you:

1) Be natural – Keep your attitude confident, not cocky
If you are not confident that you can do the job, do not expect the board to be. Do not apologize for your weaknesses, try to bring out your strong points. The board is interested in a positive, not negative, presentation. Cockiness will antagonize any board member and make him wonder if you are covering up a weakness by a false show of strength.

2) Get comfortable, but don't lounge or sprawl
Sit erectly but not stiffly. A careless posture may lead the board to conclude that you are careless in other things, or at least that you are not impressed by the importance of the occasion. Either conclusion is natural, even if incorrect. Do not fuss with your clothing, a pencil or an ashtray. Your hands may occasionally be useful to emphasize a point; do not let them become a point of distraction.

3) Do not wisecrack or make small talk
This is a serious situation, and your attitude should show that you consider it as such. Further, the time of the board is limited – they do not want to waste it, and neither should you.

4) Do not exaggerate your experience or abilities

In the first place, from information in the application or other interviews and sources, the board may know more about you than you think. Secondly, you probably will not get away with it. An experienced board is rather adept at spotting such a situation, so do not take the chance.

5) If you know a board member, do not make a point of it, yet do not hide it

Certainly you are not fooling him, and probably not the other members of the board. Do not try to take advantage of your acquaintanceship – it will probably do you little good.

6) Do not dominate the interview

Let the board do that. They will give you the clues – do not assume that you have to do all the talking. Realize that the board has a number of questions to ask you, and do not try to take up all the interview time by showing off your extensive knowledge of the answer to the first one.

7) Be attentive

You only have 20 minutes or so, and you should keep your attention at its sharpest throughout. When a member is addressing a problem or question to you, give him your undivided attention. Address your reply principally to him, but do not exclude the other board members.

8) Do not interrupt

A board member may be stating a problem for you to analyze. He will ask you a question when the time comes. Let him state the problem, and wait for the question.

9) Make sure you understand the question

Do not try to answer until you are sure what the question is. If it is not clear, restate it in your own words or ask the board member to clarify it for you. However, do not haggle about minor elements.

10) Reply promptly but not hastily

A common entry on oral board rating sheets is "candidate responded readily," or "candidate hesitated in replies." Respond as promptly and quickly as you can, but do not jump to a hasty, ill-considered answer.

11) Do not be peremptory in your answers

A brief answer is proper – but do not fire your answer back. That is a losing game from your point of view. The board member can probably ask questions much faster than you can answer them.

12) Do not try to create the answer you think the board member wants

He is interested in what kind of mind you have and how it works – not in playing games. Furthermore, he can usually spot this practice and will actually grade you down on it.

13) Do not switch sides in your reply merely to agree with a board member

Frequently, a member will take a contrary position merely to draw you out and to see if you are willing and able to defend your point of view. Do not start a debate, yet do not surrender a good position. If a position is worth taking, it is worth defending.

14) Do not be afraid to admit an error in judgment if you are shown to be wrong

The board knows that you are forced to reply without any opportunity for careful consideration. Your answer may be demonstrably wrong. If so, admit it and get on with the interview.

15) Do not dwell at length on your present job

The opening question may relate to your present assignment. Answer the question but do not go into an extended discussion. You are being examined for a *new* job, not your present one. As a matter of fact, try to phrase ALL your answers in terms of the job for which you are being examined.

Basis of Rating

Probably you will forget most of these "do's" and "don'ts" when you walk into the oral interview room. Even remembering them all will not ensure you a passing grade. Perhaps you did not have the qualifications in the first place. But remembering them will help you to put your best foot forward, without treading on the toes of the board members.

Rumor and popular opinion to the contrary notwithstanding, an oral board wants you to make the best appearance possible. They know you are under pressure – but they also want to see how you respond to it as a guide to what your reaction would be under the pressures of the job you seek. They will be influenced by the degree of poise you display, the personal traits you show and the manner in which you respond.

ABOUT THIS BOOK

This book contains tests divided into Examination Sections. Go through each test, answering every question in the margin. We have also attached a sample answer sheet at the back of the book that can be removed and used. At the end of each test look at the answer key and check your answers. On the ones you got wrong, look at the right answer choice and learn. Do not fill in the answers first. Do not memorize the questions and answers, but understand the answer and principles involved. On your test, the questions will likely be different from the samples. Questions are changed and new ones added. If you understand these past questions you should have success with any changes that arise. Tests may consist of several types of questions. We have additional books on each subject should more study be advisable or necessary for you. Finally, the more you study, the better prepared you will be. This book is intended to be the last thing you study before you walk into the examination room. Prior study of relevant texts is also recommended. NLC publishes some of these in our Fundamental Series. Knowledge and good sense are important factors in passing your exam. Good luck also helps. So now study this Passbook, absorb the material contained within and take that knowledge into the examination. Then do your best to pass that exam.

EXAMINATION SECTION

EXAMINATION SECTION
TEST 1

DIRECTIONS: Each question or incomplete statement is followed by several suggested answers or completions. Select the one that BEST answers the question or completes the statement. *PRINT THE LETTER OF THE CORRECT ANSWER IN THE SPACE AT THE RIGHT.*

Questions 1-3.

DIRECTIONS: Questions 1 through 3 are to be answered on the basis of the following paragraph.

    The Jingle-Dress dance is a popular competitive dance performed at intertribal powwows. The costume of the Jingle-Dress dancer is adorned with small metal cones. The cones are made from chewing tobacco lids, which are rolled into cylinders and sewn onto the dress. During the dance, these tin cones strike one another to produce a soft, rhythmic sound. The dancer blends complicated footwork with a series of gentle hops, causing the cones to jingle in time to the drumbeat.

1. The purpose of the cones in the Jingle-Dress dance is to   1.____

    A. shine and sparkle during the dance
    B. produce a soft, rhythmic sound
    C. aid the dancer with the complicated footwork required by the dance
    D. make use of recycled tobacco can lids

2. The dancer causes the cones to make sounds by   2.____

    A. making large cones to sew onto the dress
    B. sewing the cones as close to another as possible
    C. jumping up and down as quickly as possible
    D. combining footwork with gentle hops

3. The Jingle-Dress dance is performed as a   3.____

    A. ceremonial dance at semi-annual powwows
    B. healing dance at intertribal powwows
    C. competitive dance at intertribal powwows
    D. costume dance at annual powwows

Questions 4-6.

DIRECTIONS: Questions 4 through 6 are to be answered on the basis of the following paragraph.

    Although volleyball is a unique sport, it shares one important similarity with other well-known sports. Like most sports, the ability to win doesn't just depend on a team's ability to score the most points, but on its ability to make the fewest number of errors. In volleyball, a team cannot score unless it is serving. Serving errors, therefore, are extremely costly since losing the serve also means granting your opponent a scoring opportunity.

4. To win a volleyball game, it is MOST important to make sure your team 4.____

   A. makes the fewest number of errors
   B. plays good defense
   C. grants scoring opportunities to your opponents
   D. serves first

5. What important similarity does volleyball share with other sports? 5.____

   A. It's exciting to watch.
   B. Winning depends on a powerful serve.
   C. A volleyball team cannot score unless it is serving.
   D. The winning team usually commits the fewest errors.

6. Serving errors are costly in a volleyball game because they 6.____

   A. count as an error against your team
   B. provide your opponent with a scoring opportunity
   C. place your team in a receiving position
   D. can result in a delay-of-game penalty

Questions 7-8.

DIRECTIONS: Questions 7 and 8 are to be answered on the basis of the following paragraph.

Throughout history, solar eclipses have sometimes caused great fear and anxiety. Some cultures believed eclipses predicted the end of the world. Many older cultures believed a dragon was swallowing the sun and, in order to save the sun, people made as much noise as possible to frighten the dragon away. When the sun returned, whole and bright, the noise-makers celebrated their success.

7. Why have eclipses caused such anxiety throughout history? 7.____

   A. People believed they signaled the end of the world
   B. No one knows what causes them
   C. Because people make so much noise when they appear
   D. Because watching one can harm the eyes

8. Why did ancient cultures often make noise during an eclipse? 8.____

   A. People were frightened in the darkness
   B. To celebrate the arrival of the eclipse
   C. To summon the dragon who would swallow the sun
   D. To chase away the dragon they thought had swallowed the sun

Questions 9-11.

DIRECTIONS: Questions 9 through 11 are to be answered on the basis of the following paragraph.

In the films of the 1940s, most American Indians appeared as enemies. They spoke broken English and blocked civilization's progress. During this same time, however, a group of Navajo Indians used their unique language to develop a code for the U.S. military which would become one of the most successful codes in military history. During World War II, this group, known as the Navajo Code Talkers, played a key role in many of the most crucial victories fought by the U.S. military in the Pacific.

9. What role did the Navajo Code Talkers play in World War II? 9.____
They

    A. appeared as enemies in many films
    B. spoke broken English and blocked civilization's progress
    C. developed a military code which helped win the war in the Pacific
    D. used their unique language to block civilization's progress

10. In films from the 1940s, American Indians were most often depicted as enemies by 10.____

    A. speaking broken English and blocking civilization's progress
    B. speaking only in their native Navajo tongue
    C. using their language to develop secret codes
    D. trying to block crucial American victories in the Pacific

11. The Navajo Code Talkers used their language to 11.____

    A. block civilization's progress
    B. fight Hollywood stereotypes
    C. defeat their enemies in other tribes
    D. develop one of the most effective U.S. military codes in history

Questions 12-13.

DIRECTIONS: Questions 12 and 13 are to be answered on the basis of the following paragraph.

In the last several years, judges throughout the country have attracted controversy by practicing *creative sentencing*. The term refers to the judges' tendency for offering defendants what they consider valid alternatives to jail sentences. For example, to qualify for probation, one defendant had to wear a tee shirt that announced his status as a criminal on probation. An abusive husband had to donate his car to a shelter for battered women. In one case, a judge gave a woman found guilty of child abuse a chance to avoid jail if she would voluntarily allow Norplant, a form of birth control, to be implanted in her arm.

12. What does the term *creative sentencing* refer to? 12.____

    A. Various judicial controversies
    B. Judges who offer defendants alternatives to jail sentences

C. Defendants who are forced to undergo humiliating punishments in addition to jail sentences
D. Judges who have the power to determine how much time a defendant spends in jail

13. Creative sentencing is considered controversial because the   13.____

    A. judges are overstepping the bounds of their power by forcing defendants to submit to these punishments
    B. defendants have no opportunity to defend themselves
    C. alternatives offered to defendants are often surprising and odd
    D. judges have been forced to these extreme measures because of prison overcrowding

Questions 14-16.

DIRECTIONS: Questions 14 through 16 are to be answered on the basis of the following paragraph.

When examined closely, Earth's position in the solar system is something of a miracle. If it were closer to the sun, the heat would be so intense that water would be vaporized. If it were farther away, water would be frozen. Of all the planets in the solar system, only Earth and Mars share the temperature band which allows water to exist in the three states which are necessary to produce and sustain life. But only Earth is surrounded by a protective ozone layer which aids water in making the transition between these three states.

14. Why is Earth's position in the solar system something of a miracle?   14.____

    A. If it were closer to the sun, water would vaporize.
    B. If it were farther from the sun, water would freeze.
    C. It exists in the narrow temperature band which allows water to exist in the three states necessary to sustain life.
    D. It exists in the narrow temperature band which allows a protective ozone layer to form around the planet.

15. What is the difference between Earth and Mars?   15.____

    A. Mars is surrounded by a protective ozone layer.
    B. Earth is surrounded by a protective ozone layer.
    C. Only Earth exists within the narrow temperature band which allows water to exist in the three states necessary to sustain life.
    D. Only Mars exists within the narrow temperature band which allows water to exist in the three states necessary to sustain life.

16. The ozone layer is important to the production and sustenance of life because it   16.____

    A. helps water make the transition between the three forms necessary to sustain life
    B. keeps water from being vaporized by the sun's harmful rays
    C. keeps water from being frozen when the sun sets
    D. keeps water from leaving the atmosphere

Questions 17-19.

DIRECTIONS: Questions 17 through 19 are to be answered on the basis of the following paragraph.

During the seventeenth century, sailors at sea often suffered from muscle weakness and unexplained bleeding. This disease often proved fatal until the discovery that sailors who ate oranges and lines either didn't get sick, or suffered a much milder form of the illness. As a result, the British navy required every ship to provide lemons and limes for the entire crew. By accident, it had discovered that the vitamin C contained in the citrus fruits prevented scurvy.

17. What disease did sailors at sea often suffer from?

    A. Malnourishment
    B. Overdoses of vitamin C
    C. Muscle weakness and unexplained bleeding
    D. Scurvy

17.____

18. How is the disease prevented?

    A. Consumption of vitamin C   B. Consumption of fresh water
    C. Hard work   D. Bed rest

18.____

19. The cure for scurvy was discovered

    A. as a result of careful testing in laboratories
    B. through the accidental discovery that sailors who consumed vitamin C didn't grow ill
    C. through the accidental discovery that sailors who consumed vitamin C often grew ill
    D. as a result of years of study and experimentation

19.____

Questions 20-22.

DIRECTIONS: Questions 20 through 22 are to be answered on the basis of the following paragraph.

Unlike dogs, cats are typically a solitary animal species who avoid social interaction, but they do display specific social responses to each other upon meeting. When two cats meet who are strangers, their first actions and gestures determine who the *dominant* cat will be. If a cat desires dominance or sees the other cat as a threat to its territory, it will stare directly at the intruder with a lowered tail. If the other cat responds with a similar gesture, or with the strong defensive posture of an arched back, laid-back ears, and raised tail, a fight or chase is likely if neither cat gives in. This is unlikely, however; before such a point of open hostility is reached, one of the cats will usually take the *submissive* position of crouching down while looking away from the other cat.

20. A cat signals its dominance over another cat by

    A. crouching down and looking away from the other cat
    B. arching its back and raising its tail
    C. staring directly at the other cat and lowering its tail
    D. chasing the other cat

20.____

21. Cats usually greet each other by 21.____

    A. displaying specific social responses
    B. staring directly at one another
    C. raising their tails
    D. arching their backs

22. Why is it unlikely for cats who are strangers to reach a point of open hostility with one another? 22.____

    A. Cats are solitary animals.
    B. One of the cats usually runs away.
    C. One of the cats usually takes a submissive position before they reach the point of open hostility.
    D. The two cats generally stare at each other with lowered tails until the hostility passes.

Questions 23-25.

DIRECTIONS: Questions 23 through 25 are to be answered on the basis of the following paragraph.

Between the nineteenth and twentieth centuries, the area in America known as the Great Plains underwent startling changes. At the beginning of the nineteenth century, there were few settlements. One could walk for miles without seeing a house. By the end of the century, settlements had sprung up all over. More and more people began to seek their fortunes in this area. In 1800, the Plains were covered by herds of buffalo. These huge animals were the natural cattle of the Plains. By 1900 the buffalo had almost disappeared, however, and the tribes who had roamed the Plains in pursuit of the buffalo had been forced to live on reservations.

23. When did these changes occur on the Great Plains? 23.____

    A. Between the 1700s and the 1800s
    B. Between the 1800s and the 1900s
    C. During the 1900s
    D. Between 1850 and 1950

24. What caused the sudden increase in the number of settlements on the Great Plains? 24.____

    A. The disappearance of the buffalo
    B. The disappearance of the Plains tribes
    C. An increased desire to hunt buffalo for sport
    D. An increased number of people seeking their fortunes in the area

25. What happened to the Plains tribes after the buffalo disappeared? 25.____
    They

    A. were forced to live on reservations
    B. were all killed
    C. died of starvation
    D. moved farther west, away from the settlers

Questions 26-28.

DIRECTIONS: Questions 26 through 28 are to be answered on the basis of the following paragraph.

One important line of thinking about stress focuses on the differences between Type A and Type B personalities. Type A individuals are extremely competitive, are very devoted to work, and have a strong sense of time urgency. They are likely to be aggressive, impatient, and very work-oriented. Type B individuals are less competitive, less devoted to work, and have a weaker sense of time urgency. These individuals are less likely to experience conflict with other people and more likely to have a balanced, relaxed approach to life.

26. Type B individuals are likely to display which of the following characteristics? 26.____

    A. A strong sense of time urgency
    B. Devotion to work
    C. A balanced approach to life
    D. Aggressiveness

27. Type A individuals are likely to display which of the following characteristics? 27.____

    A. A balanced approach to life
    B. Passivity
    C. Contentment
    D. A strong sense of time urgency

28. These personality types help researchers study which of the following problems? 28.____

    A. Stress
    B. Apathy
    C. Criminal behavior
    D. Underachievement

Questions 29-36.

The paragraphs which follow contain blank spaces with numbers corresponding to the questions. Each of the corresponding questions contains one lettered choice whose meaning fits in the space. Place the letter of the correct choice in the answer space to the right of the question.

Most successful job interviews (29) three basic steps. Step 1 lasts about three minutes and (30) when you first introduce yourself. Those people who have a firm handshake, who maintain eye contact, smile, and seem friendly, are the (31) successful during this phase. Step 2 is the (32) phase. This is the point at which interviewees (33) their skills and work to *sell* themselves. Step 3 comes at the (34) of the interview and, like Step 1, lasts only a few minutes. After the employer says, *We'll call you,* successful interviewees are quick (35) respond, *I'll get in touch with you if I don't hear from you in a few days.* This final gesture conveys (36).

29.	A. lack C. follow	B. mimic D. end with			29.___
30.	A. begins	B. ends	C. stalls	D. fails	30.___
31.	A. least	B. mostly	C. more	D. most	31.___
32.	A. least challenging C. longest	B. most boring D. shortest			32.___
33.	A. brag about	B. explain	C. enunciate	D. lie about	33.___
34.	A. middle	B. outset	C. beginning	D. end	34.___
35.	A. to	B. at	C. with	D. for	35.___
36.	A. insistence C. enthusiasm	B. impatience D. hope			36.___

Questions 37-40.

The idea of duty is important to the followers of Hinduism, the major (37) in India. In fact, the many duties prescribed by Hinduism make it a way of life that (38) each day. From an early age, children learn that nothing is more important (39) doing one's duty. In fact doing (40) duty is, in itself, a form of worship.

37.	A. belief C. system	B. religion D. political institution			37.___
38.	A. organizes C. produces	B. disrupts D. destabilizes			38.___
39.	A. if	B. with	C. of	D. than	39.___
40.	A. your	B. his	C. one's	D. its	40.___

Questions 41-46.

Strong emotions are accompanied (41) physiological changes. When we are extremely fearful or angry, for example, (42) heartbeat speeds up, our pulse races, and our breathing rate tends to increase. The body's metabolism (43), burning up sugar in the bloodstream and fats in the tissues at a faster rate. The salivary glands become less active, making the mouth feel (44). The sweat glands may overreact, (45) a dripping forehead, clammy hands, and cold sweat. Finally, the pupils may (46), producing the wide-eyed look that is characteristic of both terror and rage.

41.	A. with	B. to	C. beside	D. by	41.___
42.	A. your	B. our	C. the	D. a	42.___

43.	A. accelerates	B. slows down	43.____
	C. works	D. stays the same	

44.	A. hot	B. cold	C. wet	D. dry	44.____

45.	A. with	B. showing	C. producing	D. fearing	45.____

46.	A. dilate	B. enlarge	C. blacken	D. disappear	46.____

Questions 47-52.

Increased numbers of women are (47) going to college and graduating with degrees in law and medicine. More women than ever before are (48) careers and earning as much as men. Many career women who are married have also achieved economic equality (49) their husbands. The number of women in elected office has also increased, and a large majority of Americans are now willing to vote for a qualified (50) for president. A growing number of women are entering the military, with the U.S. now having more female soldiers than any other (51). These are all signs that women have made significant headway toward (52) equality.

47.	A. now	B. then	C. yet	D. not	47.____
48.	A. leaving	B. changing	C. avoiding	D. pursuing	48.____
49.	A. to	B. with	C. at	D. for	49.____
50.	A. Republican	B. candidate	C. woman	D. man	50.____
51.	A. woman	B. country	C. man	D. branch	51.____
52.	A. racial	B. economic	C. religious	D. gender	52.____

Questions 53-56.

Understanding does not mean manipulating someone to agree (53) your point of view. Although a manipulative person views understanding as having someone else come around to his or her opinion, an understanding person conveys a sense of open-mindedness and (54). A communicator who is understanding does (55) insist upon agreement. He or she understands that, in order to be understood, you must also (56) others.

53.	A. to	B. at	C. with	D. for	53.____
54.	A. acceptance	B. exclusion	C. anger	D. elation	54.____
55.	A. always	B. not	C. sometimes	D. generally	55.____

56.	A. disagree with	B. judge	56.____
	C. love	D. understand	

Questions 57-62.

DIRECTIONS: Questions 57 through 62 are to be answered on the basis of the following facts.

Apollo Elementary School serves students in grades kindergarten through fifth. The school library is located in the center of the school. Classrooms surround the library, forming a large circle. Throughout the school day, teachers bring their classes into the library to conduct research and reading activities. There are usually several classes using the library at any one time.

The school librarian is Mrs. Samuels. She is a tall, middle-aged woman with brown hair and green eyes. Her part-time assistant is Velma Thomas. Velma is a student at the local community college, where she studies library science.

On the afternoon of Wednesday, April 11, Mrs. Simon brought her fourth-grade class to the library at approximately 1:50 P.M. Mrs. Samuels was already working with a third-grade class, so Velma began assisting the fourth grade students. A young girl from Mrs. Simon's class asked Velma how to find her book in the card catalog. As Velma guided the girl through the procedure, she noticed that one of the third graders had drifted away from his class and was attempting to reach a book by standing on one of the bookshelves.

Just as Velma called to the boy, he lost his footing and fell. Mrs. Samuels rushed to his side and checked him for injuries. The boy had a slight bruise on his wrist, but was otherwise uninjured.

57. Who checked the boy for injuries after his fall?

   A. Mrs. Samuels
   B. Velma Thomas
   C. Mrs. Simon
   D. The third grade teacher

58. Who is the school librarian?

   A. Mrs. Samuels
   B. Velma Thomas
   C. Mrs. Simon
   D. She is not named in this passage

59. On what day of the week did the incident occur?

   A. Monday   B. Tuesday   C. Wednesday   D. Friday

60. In what grade was the boy who fell from the shelf?

   A. Fifth   B. Fourth   C. Third   D. Second

61. What grade does Mrs. Simon teach?

   A. Fifth   B. Fourth   C. Third   D. Second

62. What grades does Apollo Elementary serve? 62.____

   A. First through fifth
   B. First through sixth
   C. Kindergarten through fourth
   D. Kindergarten through fifth

Questions 63-68.

DIRECTIONS: Questions 63 through 68 are to be answered on the basis of the following facts.

There is a small hot dog cart located in the outdoor plaza of the Smith County Courthouse. The cart sells Polish hot dogs, sausages, bratwurst, soft pretzels, and soda. In the mornings between 7:00 and 9:30, fresh coffee and danishes are also sold. Employees of the court and other nearby businesses often purchase their lunch there, and eat on the plaza benches and tables.

The cart opens at 7:00 A.M. and closes at 3:00 P.M. during weekdays. It does not operate on weekends. It is owned and operated by Luisa Gonzalez, who is a 21-year-old college student with brown hair and brown eyes. Her father is Martin Gonzalez, a retired police officer, and he often works with her. At approximately 12:00 P.M. on October 3, Court Officer Laura Innes stopped at the cart to buy her lunch. After paying Luisa, Laura moved to the condiment table, located just to the right of the cart. She noticed Martin Gonzalez struggling to pour a large tub of boiling water into the hot dog steamer. Before she could move to help him, however, Martin lost his grip and dropped the tub of water, splashing himself.

The Court Officer administered first aid, and Martin was taken to St. Luke's hospital. He had received second degree burns on his arms and feet and was not able to return to the hot dog cart for three weeks.

63. What hospital was Martin taken to? 63.____

   A. St. Mark' s   B. St. Peter' s
   C. St. Mary' s   D. St. Luke' s

64. What part of his body did Martin burn? 64.____
   His

   A. arms and feet   B. arms
   C. feet and ankles   D. arms and face

65. Who owns the hot dog cart? 65.____

   A. Martin Gonzalez   B. Luisa Gonzalez
   C. Laura Innes   D. Luke Martin

66. During what hours does the cart operate on weekends? 66.____

   A. 7:00 A.M. to 3:00 P.M.
   B. 9:30 A.M. to 3:00 P.M.
   C. 7:00 A.M. to 9:30 A.M.
   D. The cart does not operate on weekends

67. Where is the hot dog cart located?
    On the _____ of the courthouse.

    A. first floor
    B. roof
    C. outdoor plaza
    D. third floor

68. Who was first to administer first aid to Martin?

    A. Laura Innes
    B. Luisa Gonzalez
    C. Luke Martin
    D. Paramedics

Questions 69-74.

DIRECTIONS: Questions 69 through 74 are to be answered on the basis of the following facts.

The offices of Judge Anjelica Chen are located on the third floor of the Peak County Courthouse. The offices of Judge Benjamin Laurence are also located on the third floor of the courthouse, across a courtyard. The windows of these offices face one another.

Judge Chen keeps her pet parrot, Mabel, in her offices. Although Mabel has a cage, Judge Chen keeps the door open, allowing Mabel to perch on bookshelves and lamps while the Judge finishes paperwork late in the evenings. Judge Laurence has no pets, but he often feeds pigeons from his window, sprinkling breadcrumbs along his sill.

On the evening of Tuesday, May 2, Court Officer Roger Crawford heard a scream from Judge Chen's office. He arrived to find the judge searching frantically through her office for Mabel, who had apparently disappeared. The window to the judge's office was open. The court officer assisted the judge in her search. At approximately 7:30, nearly 45 minutes after he had arrived in Judge Chen's office, the court officer heard someone hollering from the other side of the building.

Officer Crawford rushed toward the noise and found Judge Laurence in his office, trying to fend off the bright parrot flying back and forth across his office. The court officer summoned Judge Chen, who calmed Mabel and led her back to her cage.

69. Where was Mabel found?

    A. In Judge Chen's office
    B. In Judge Laurence's office
    C. In the courtyard
    D. In her cage

70. What kind of bird is Mabel?

    A. Pigeon   B. Canary   C. Chickadee   D. Parrot

71. Where is Judge Chen's office located?
    _____ Judge Laurence's office.

    A. Below   B. Next to   C. Across from   D. Above

72. Why does Judge Laurence leave breadcrumbs on his window-sill?   72._____

    A. To feed pigeons
    B. To feed Mabel
    C. To feed squirrels
    D. To keep food litter out of his office

73. How long did Judge Chen and Officer Crawford look for Mabel before they heard Judge   73._____
    Laurence yelling in his office?
    _____ minutes.

    A. 30   B. 45   C. 60   D. 15

74. Why does Judge Chen leave Mabel's cage door open?   74._____

    A. To allow Mabel to escape
    B. To allow Mabel a clearer view of Judge Laurence's windowsill
    C. Judge Chen does not leave Mabel's cage door open
    D. To allow Mabel to perch on bookshelves and lamps while the Judge finishes her paperwork

Questions 75-80.

DIRECTIONS: Questions 75 through 80 are to be answered on the basis of the following facts.

The Hickory Ridge Courthouse is located just across the street from the Hickory Ridge Public Library. Employees begin arriving at the courthouse at approximately 7:00 A.M. each weekday morning. The library opens at 9:00 A.M. and closes at 5:00 P.M. each weekday. Both the courthouse and the library have bicycle stands in front of them. Bicyclists lock their bikes to the stands while they run their errands and conduct their business.

Court Officer Melinda Thompson eats her lunch each day at a small cafe next to the library. The cafe caters mainly to employees of the library and courthouse. It operates from 11:00 A.M. to 3:00 P.M. each day.

On the afternoon of August 11, the court officer observed a young man with a backpack lock his bike to a stand in front of the library. The young man had blond hair, green eyes, and long sideburns. Approximately 30 minutes after the young man entered the library, a dark-haired man emerged from the cafe where the court officer was eating her lunch. The man had a beard, and was of medium build. He walked to the bicycle stand and began jiggling a lock on one of the bikes.

The court officer recognized the bicycle as the same one the blond-haired young man had locked to the stand. By the time the court officer reached the bicycle stand, the second man had already broken the lock. Although she called for him to stop, he rode away on the young man's bicycle. Her excellent description, however, helped police locate the bicycle thief and the bicycle a short time later.

75. What time does the library open?   75._____

    A. 7:00 A.M.   B. 9:00 A.M.   C. 11:00 A.M.   D. 3:00 P.M.

76. Where is the cafe located? 76.____

    A. Next to the courthouse
    B. Across from the library
    C. Next to the library
    D. Between the library and the courthouse

77. Who stole the bicycle? 77.____

    A. The blond-haired man
    B. The dark-haired man
    C. The man with the backpack
    D. The man with the long sideburns

78. What hours is the cafe open? 78.____

    A. 11:00 A.M. to 3:00 P.M.   B. 9:00 A.M. to 5:00 P.M.
    C. 7:00 A.M. to 5:00 P.M.   D. 7:00 A.M. to 3:00 P.M.

79. When do employees begin arriving at the courthouse each day? 79.____

    A. 7:00 A.M.   B. 9:00 A.M.   C. 10:00 A.M.   D. 11:00 A.M.

80. What did the bicycle thief do when the court officer ordered him to stop? 80.____

    A. He stopped.
    B. He rode away.
    C. He threw down the bicycle and ran.
    D. He insisted the bicycle was his.

Questions 81-87.

DIRECTIONS: Questions 81 through 87 are to be answered on the basis of the following facts.

The Jade Market is located on the first floor of the Angel County Courthouse. The courthouse is located across the street from San Gabriel High School. Jade Market sells newspapers, magazines, sandwiches, beverages, and sodas. In the mornings, between 7:00 A.M. and 9:00 A.M., the market is frequented mostly by employees of the courthouse. In the afternoons, between 1:45 and 2:45, the small market is crowded with teenagers wearing cumbersome backpacks. Classes at San Gabriel High School end at 1:30 P.M.

Jade Market is operated by James Chang, who is 55 years old, with graying black hair and brown eyes. His wife, Lola, also helps at the market during the afternoon and evening hours.

On the afternoon of Thursday, September 1, Court Officer Mason Stewart stopped at Jade Market to buy a newspaper and some coffee. While he was talking with Lola Chang, twelve to fifteen high school students walked into the market. They moved noisily up and down the narrow aisles. They each carried a heavy backpack. As they walked through the store, their packs often knocked items from the shelves.

As the court officer watched the students, he noticed one young woman knock several magazines from the magazine stand located at the back of the store. Several other students walked past the magazine stand before the young woman was able to turn around and pick the magazines up. The young woman had blond hair and brown eyes, and she carried a red backpack. When she returned to the stand, Officer Stewart saw that she only replaced one magazine.

When the court officer approached the girl about the missing magazines, she insisted that she had not seen them. He asked her to wait at the front counter, which she did. Officer Stewart studied the magazine stand for a brief moment, and then bent down to peer beneath it. He saw the magazines lying there, where they had been accidentally kicked by the other passing students. The young woman helped gather the magazines, and then left the store after apologizing to Mr. and Mrs. Chang.

81. What hours is the market open?

    A. 7:00 A.M. to 2:45 P.M.
    B. 7:00 A.M. to 9:00 A.M.
    C. 7:00 A.M. to 1:30 P.M.
    D. The passage doesn't contain this information

81.____

82. Where were the missing magazines found?

    A. Inside the girl's backpack
    B. On the magazine stand
    C. Beneath the magazine stand
    D. They were never found

82.____

83. What did the girl do when Officer Stewart asked her about the missing magazines? She

    A. ran from the store
    B. denied stealing them
    C. confessed
    D. ran to the front counter

83.____

84. Where is the Jade Market located?

    A. On the first floor of the courthouse
    B. On the third floor of the courthouse
    C. Next to Angel High School
    D. In the plaza of Angel High School

84.____

85. When does Lola Chang work in the market?

    A. All day
    B. Afternoons
    C. Afternoons and evenings
    D. The passage doesn't contain this information

85.____

86. On what day of the week did the incident occur?

    A. Monday   B. Tuesday   C. Wednesday   D. Thursday

86.____

87. What time are students at San Gabriel High School dismissed from class? 87.____

   A. 1:30 P.M.
   B. 1:45 P.M.
   C. 2:45 P.M.
   D. The passage does not contain this information

Questions 88-89.

DIRECTIONS: Questions 88 and 89 are to be answered on the basis of the following facts.

Procedure: The Service Station at the Friendly Car Dealership has a policy which allows customers to drop off their cars the night before they are to be worked on. This allows customers the convenience of not having to take time off from work to have their cars serviced. Cars must be dropped off between 9 P.M. and 11 P.M. the night before. Keys must be labeled with the make and license plate number of the car to which they belong. They are then placed into envelopes and dropped into a locked drop box outside the service station office. Cars must be picked up by 9:00 P.M. on the day repairs are completed. If the car cannot be picked up on that day, other arrangements must be made with the service department by 3:00 P.M. of that day.

Situation: Sarah Stone drops her car off at 10:45 P.M. the night before it is to be serviced. She labels her key, places it in the envelope and leaves it in the drop box. Her car is repaired by 11:00 A.M. the next morning. Because Sarah has to catch up on a backlog of work, she is unable to pick her car up before 6:00 P.M. on the day after the repairs have been completed.

88. Based on the above procedure, which one of the following statements regarding Stone's 88.____
    actions is correct?
    Stone

   A. should have dropped her car off before 10:45 P.M. the night before it was to be serviced
   B. should have given her keys to someone in the service department instead of dropping them in a box
   C. should have notified the service department of her plans by 3:00 P.M. on the day the car was repaired
   D. did everything according to proper procedure

89. If Stone wishes to pick her car up at 8:00 P.M. the day the repairs are completed, which 89.____
    of the following things must she do?
    She

   A. must make special arrangements with the service department
   B. must wait until the following morning to pick up her car
   C. must make a special appointment to pick up her car after hours
   D. does not need to do anything

Questions 90-91.

DIRECTIONS: Questions 90 and 91 are to be answered on the basis of the following facts.

Procedure: Notification of absence due to illness must be made between 9:00 A.M. and 10:00 A.M. on the first day of illness. Illness which results in more than four days of consecutive absence must be confirmed by a doctor's note stating the nature of the illness and the approximate date of return to work.

Situation: Officer Janus Lee becomes sick on the night of June 25 while at home. At 10:15 on the morning of June 26, Lee notifies his office that he will not be in. On July 4, Lee submits a doctor's note confirming and identifying his illness and stating that Lee will return to work on July 5.

90. Based on the above procedure, which one of the following statements regarding Lee's actions is correct?
Officer Lee

    A. should have notified his office of his absence by 10:00 A.M. on the morning of June 26
    B. should have notified his office of his absence by 10:00 A.M. on the morning of June 25
    C. should have submitted the doctor's note on June 26
    D. followed the procedure correctly

91. Officer Lee's note from the doctor states that he will be absent from the office from June 26 through July 4. Which of the following notification procedures should he follow on those days?

    A. Officer Lee must notify his office of his absence on each morning between June 26 and July 4 by 10:00 A.M.
    B. Officer Lee's doctor must notify his office of Officer Lee's absence on each morning between June 26 and July 4 by 10:00 A.M.
    C. Officer Lee must contact his office periodically between June 26 and July 4 to notify them of his progress.
    D. Once he has submitted his doctor's note, Officer Lee does not need to notify his office any further so long as he returns to work on July 5.

Questions 92-93.

DIRECTIONS: Questions 92 and 93 are to be answered on the basis of the following facts.

Procedure: Court officers in Montgomery County who work overtime are awarded compensation time instead of overtime pay. Each hour of over-time is equal to one hour of compensation time. In order to use compensation time, court officers must submit a written vacation request two weeks in advance of the desired time off. The request must contain the beginning and ending dates of the requested vacation. It must be signed by the officer's supervisor before the officer may utilize the compensation time.

Situation: Officer Sabrina Hellman wishes to use compensation time for a vacation beginning October 1 and ending October 10. The vacation will require 7 days of compensation time. Officer Hellman submits her vacation request on September 24. The request contains the beginning and ending dates of her desired vacation.

92. Based on the above procedure, which of the following statements regarding Officer Hellman's actions is correct?
Officer Hellman

   A. should have submitted her vacation request by September 17
   B. should have submitted her vacation request by September 1
   C. should have submitted the beginning and ending dates of her vacation
   D. followed the procedures correctly

93. How many hours of overtime must Officer Hellman have in order to accumulate 100 hours of compensation time?

   A. 50   B. 75   C. 150   D. 100

Questions 94-95.

DIRECTIONS: Questions 94 and 95 are to be answered on the basis of the following facts.

Procedure: Court officers in Salinas County who work overtime are awarded compensation time instead of overtime pay. Each hour of overtime is equal to one hour of compensation time. At the end of each calendar year, compensation time which has not been used is automatically erased unless employees submit a written request to have their compensation time rolled over to the next year. Rollover requests must be submitted no later than November 1. They must contain the employee's name, social security, and the total number of compensation hours s/he wishes to rollover.

Situation: Officer Larry Bernstein accumulated 20 hours of compensation time during calendar year 2008. In addition to that, he has 40 hours of compensation time which was rolled over from 2007. On October 30, Officer Bernstein submits a written request asking that his remaining compensation time be rolled over to calendar year 2009.

94. Based on the above procedure, which of the following statements regarding Officer Bernstein's actions is correct? Officer Bernstein

   A. should have submitted his rollover request by November 1, 2008
   B. should have submitted his vacation request by October 1, 2008
   C. should have submitted the total number of hours he wanted to be rolled over
   D. followed the procedures correctly

95. Based on the above procedure and situation, how many hours of compensation time can Officer Bernstein expect to be rolled over to calendar year 2009?

   A. 20   B. 40   C. 60   D. 80

Questions 96-97.

DIRECTIONS: Questions 96 and 97 are to be answered on the basis of the following facts.

Procedure: Court officers in Salinas County who work overtime are awarded compensation time instead of overtime pay. Each hour of overtime is equal to one hour of compensation time. If a court officer is laid off or chooses to leave his or her employment as a court officer with the county, and he or she has compensation time remaining, then he or she can choose one of two options. The first option is for the employee to use the remaining compensation time as paid vacation time. This would allow the officer to cease his or her duties early, but still be paid until the end of his or her regular employment. In order to utilize this option, employees must submit a written request 30 days before the start of the paid vacation. The second option is for the employee to remain through the end of his or her regular employment, and receive a check for any remaining compensation time. In order to utilize this option, employees must submit a written request 90 days before the scheduled departure date.

Situation: Officer Glen Regan is due to retire at the end of calendar year 2008. Through the course of his career as a court officer, Glen has accumulated 200 hours of compensation time. This equals approximately 25 standard working days.

96. If Officer Regan decides that he would like to retire early, he should submit a written request by _____ 1, 2008.

    A. December   B. November   C. October   D. September

97. If Officer Regan decides to receive a check for his unused compensation time, he should submit a written request by _____ 1, 2008.

    A. December   B. November   C. October   D. September

Questions 98-100.

DIRECTIONS: Questions 98 through 100 are to be answered on the basis of the following facts.

Procedure: Court officers in James County are granted 10 paid sick days each year. Sick days are to be used only in the case of unforeseen illness. Employees are also granted 5 paid personal days. Officers who work overtime are also granted compensation time instead of overtime pay. Each hour of overtime is equal to one hour of compensation time. In order to use a sick day, employees must notify a supervisor by 10:00 A.M. on the day of their absence. In order to use a personal day, employees must notify a supervisor two working days in advance. In order to use a compensation-time day, employees must notify a supervisor two weeks in advance.

Situation: Court Officer Carla Lewis has a doctor and a dentist appointment on Monday, October 5.

98. In order to use a compensation day for these appointments, by what date must Carla notify her supervisor?

    A. Friday, September 4   B. Monday, September 14
    C. 10:00 A.M. October 5   D. Thursday, September 1

99. If Officer Carla Lewis wants to use a personal day for these appointments, by what date must she notify her supervisor?

    A. Friday, September 4   B. Monday, September 14
    C. 10:00 A.M. October 5   D. Thursday, October 1

100. If Officer Carla Lewis wants to use a sick day for these appointments, by what date must she notify her supervisor? 100.____

    A. 10:00 A.M. on October 5
    B. Monday, September 14
    C. She cannot use a sick day for these appointments
    D. She does not have to notify her supervisor until after she returns to work

KEY (CORRECT ANSWERS)

1.	B	21.	A	41.	D	61.	B	81.	D
2.	D	22.	C	42.	B	62.	D	82.	C
3.	C	23.	B	43.	A	63.	D	83.	B
4.	A	24.	D	44.	D	64.	A	84.	A
5.	D	25.	A	45.	C	65.	B	85.	C
6.	B	26.	C	46.	B	66.	D	86.	D
7.	A	27.	D	47.	A	67.	C	87.	A
8.	D	28.	A	48.	D	68.	A	88.	C
9.	C	29.	C	49.	B	69.	B	89.	D
10.	A	30.	A	50.	C	70.	D	90.	A
11.	D	31.	D	51.	B	71.	C	91.	D
12.	B	32.	C	52.	D	72.	A	92.	A
13.	C	33.	B	53.	C	73.	B	93.	D
14.	C	34.	D	54.	A	74.	D	94.	D
15.	B	35.	A	55.	B	75.	B	95.	C
16.	A	36.	C	56.	D	76.	C	96.	B
17.	D	37.	B	57.	A	77.	B	97.	C
18.	A	38.	A	58.	A	78.	A	98.	B
19.	B	39.	D	59.	C	79.	A	99.	D
20.	C	40.	C	60.	C	80.	B	100.	C

EXAMINATION SECTION

TEST 1

DIRECTIONS: Each question or incomplete statement is followed by several suggested answers or completions. Select the one that BEST answers the question or completes the statement. *PRINT THE LETTER OF THE CORRECT ANSWER IN THE SPACE AT THE RIGHT.*

Questions 1-4 are based solely on the information in the paragraph below:

A Court Officer shall give reasonable aid to a sick or injured person. He or she shall summon an ambulance, if necessary, by telephoning the Police Department, which shall notify the hospital. He or she shall wait in a place where the arriving ambulance can see him or her, if possible, so as to direct the ambulance attendant to the patient. If the ambulance does not arrive within a half-hour, the Court Officer should call a second time, telling the department that this is a second call. However, if the injured person is conscious, the Court Officer should ask whether such person is willing to go to a hospital before calling for an ambulance.

1. The Court Officer who wishes to summon an ambulance should telephone the
    A. nearest hospital
    B. Health and Hospitals Corporation
    C. Police Department
    D. nearest police precinct

    1._____

2. If an ambulance does not arrive within half an hour, the Court Officer should
    A. ask the person injured if he/she wants to go to the hospital in a cab
    B. call the Police Department
    C. call the nearest police precinct
    D. call the nearest hospital

    2._____

3. A Court Officer who is called to help a person who has fallen on the courthouse steps and apparently has a broken leg should
    A. put the leg in traction so the doctor will have no difficulty setting it
    B. ask the person, if he/she is conscious, whether he/she wishes to go to the hospital
    C. attempt to get the story behind the injury
    D. put in a call for an ambulance at once

    3._____

4. A Court Officer who is present when a witness becomes ill while waiting to testify should
    A. wait in front of the room until the ambulance arrives
    B. send a bystander to the courtroom to page a doctor
    C. ask the withness if he/she wishes to go to a hospital
    D. call the Court Clerk for instructions

    4._____

5. "Physical and mental health are essential to the Court Officer."
   According to this statement, a peace officer must be
   A. wise as well as strong
   B. smarter than most people
   C. sound in mind and body
   D. smarter than the average criminal

6. "Teamwork is the basis of successful law enforcement."
   The factor stressed by this statement is
   A. cooperation
   B. determination
   C. initiative
   D. pride

7. "A sufficient quantity of material supplied as evidence enables the laboratory expert to determine the true nature of the substance, whereas an extremely limited specimen may be an abnormal sample containing foreign matter not indicative of the true nature of the material."
   On the basis of this statement alone, it may be concluded that a reason for giving an adequate sample of material for evidence to a laboratory expert is that
   A. a limited specimen spoils more quickly than a larger sample
   B. a small sample may not truly represent the evidence
   C. he or she cannot analyze a small sample correctly
   D. he or she must have enough material to keep a part of it untouched to show in court

8. "The Housing Authority not only faces every problem of the private developer, it must also assume responsibilities of which a private building is free. The authority must account to the community; it must conform to Federal regulations and it must overcome the prejudices of contractors, bankers and prospective tenants against public operations. These authorities are being watched for the first error of judgment or the first evidence of high costs that can be torn to bits before a congressional committee."
   On the basis of this selection, which statement would be most correct?
   A. Private builders do not have the opposition of contractors, bankers and prospective tenants
   B. Congressional committees impede the progress of public housing by petty investigations
   C. A housing authority must deal with all the difficulties encountered by the private builder
   D. Housing authorities are not more immune to errors in judgment than private developers

9. Accident proneness is a subject that deserves much more objective and competent study than it has received to date. In discussing accident proneness, it is important to differentiate between the employee who is a "repeater" and one who is truly accident-prone. It is obvious that any person assigned to work without thorough training is liable to injury until he or she does learn the "how" of it. Few workers left to their own devices develop adequate safe practices, and therefore they must be trained. Only those who fail to respond to proper training should be regarded as accident-prone. The repeater whose accident record can be explained by a correctable physical defect, correctable plant or machine hazards, or by assignment to work for which he or she is not suited because of physical deficiencies or special abilities cannot be fairly called accident-prone.
   According to the passage, people are considered accident-prone if
   A. they have accidents regardless of the fact that they have been properly trained
   B. they have many accidents
   C. it is possible for them to have accidents
   D. they work at a job where accidents are possible

9._____

Questions 10 through 12 are based on the following paragraph:

Discontent of some citizens with the practices and policies of local government leads to the creation of local civic associations. Completely outside of government, manned by a few devoted volunteers, understaffed, and with pitifully few dues-paying members, they attempt to arouse widespread public opinion on selected issues by presenting facts and ideas. The findings of these civic associations are widely trusted by the press and public, and amidst the records of rebuffs received are found more than enough achievements to justify what little their activities cost. Civic associations are politically non-partisan. Hence their vitality is drawn from true political independents who in most communities are a trifling minority. Except in a few large cities, civic associations are seldom affluent enough to maintain an office or to afford even a small paid staff.

10. The main reason for the formation of civic associations is to
    A. provide independent candidates for local public office with an opportunity to be heard
    B. bring about changes in the activities of local government
    C. allow persons who are politically non-partisan to express themselves on local public issues
    D. permit the small minority of true political independents to supply leadership for non-partisan causes

10._____

11. The statements that civic associations make on issues of general interest are
    A. accepted by large segments of the public
    B. taken at face value only by the few people who are true political independents
    C. questioned as to their accuracy by most newspapers
    D. expressed as a result of aroused widespread public opinion

11._____

12. It is most accurate to conclude that since
    A. they deal with many public issues, the cost of their efforts on each issue is small
    B. their attempts to attain their objectives often fail, little money is contributed to civic associations
    C. they spend little money in their efforts, they are ineffective when they become involved in major issues
    D. their achievements outweigh the small cost of their efforts, civic associations are considered worthwhile

13. "If you are in doubt as to whether any matter is properly mailable, you should ask the postmaster. Even though the post office has not expressly declared any matter to be nonmailable, the sender of such matter may be held fully liable for violation of law if he does actually send nonmailable matter through the mails."
    Of the following, the most accurate statement made concerning this selection is
    A. nonmailable matter is not always clearly defined
    B. ignorance of what constitutes nonmailable matter relieves the sender of all responsibility
    C. though doubt may exist about the mailability of any matter, the sender is fully liable for any law violation if such matter should be nonmailable
    D. the post office is not explicit in its position on the violation of the nonmailable matter law

Questions 14 through 16 are based on the following paragraph:

What is required is a program that will protect our citizens and their property from criminal and anti-social acts, will effectively restrain and reform juvenile delinquents, and will prevent the further development of anti-social behavior. Discipline and punishment of offenders must necessarily play an important part in any such program. Serious offenders cannot be mollycoddled merely because they are under 21. Restraint and punishment necessarily follow serious anti-social acts. But punishment, if it is to be effective, must be a planned part of a more comprehensive program of treating delinquency.

14. The one goal not included among those listed in the paragraph is to
    A. stop young people from defacing public property
    B. keep homes from being broken into
    C. develop an intra-city boys baseball league
    D. change juvenile delinquents into useful citizens

15. Punishment is
    A. not satisfactory in any program dealing with juvenile delinquents
    B. the most effective means by which young vandals and hooligans can be reformed
    C. not used sufficiently when dealing with serious offenders who are under 21
    D. of value in reducing juvenile delinquency only if it is part of a complete program

16. With respect to serious offenders who are under 21 years of age, the paragraph suggests that they
    A. be mollycoddled
    B. be dealt with as part of a comprehensive program to punish mature criminals
    C. should be punished
    D. be prevented, by brute force if necessary, from performing anti-social acts

16._____

17. Statistics tell us that heart disease kills more people than any other illness, and the death rate continues to rise. People over 30 have a 50-50 chance of escaping, for heart disease is chiefly an illness of people in late middle age and advanced years. Since more people in this age group are living today than were some years ago, heart disease is able to find more victims.
On the basis of this selection, the statement which is most nearly correct is that
    A. half the people over 30 years of age have heart disease today
    B. more people die of heart disease than of all other diseases combined
    C. older people are the chief victims of heart disease
    D. the rising birth rate has increased the possibility that the average person will die of heart disease

17._____

18. Assume that a Court Officer is allowed 25 cents a mile for the use of her automobile for the purpose of conducting defendants to and from court sessions. The first month she drove 416 miles; the second month 328 miles; the third month 2,012 miles; the fourth month 187 miles; the fifth month 713 miles; the sixth month 1,608 miles. Her expenditures for gasoline averaged $2.70 a gallon and her general average of miles per gallon was 16; she used 32 quarts of oil at $1.25 per quart and spent $351.20 on care and general upkeep of her car for the six months. Without considering the depreciation in value of her car, she would have received above her expenditures:
    A. $36.50
    B. $40
    C. $96.10
    D. $263.20

18._____

19. Assume that you borrowed $2,000 on Nov. 1, 1999, for the use of which you were required to pay simple interest semi-annually at seven percent a year. By May 1, 2005, you would have paid interest amounting to
    A. $140
    B. $280
    C. $700
    D. $770

19._____

20. A courtroom contains 72 persons, which is two-fifths of its capacity. The number of persons that the courtroom can hold is
    A. 28   B. 129   C. 180   D. 200-300

20._____

21. The total cost of 30 pencils at 18 cents a dozen, 12 paper pads at 27-1/2 cents each and eight boxes of paper clips at 5-1/4 cents a box is
    A. more than $10
    B. $1.50
    C. $4.17
    D. $1.52

    21._____

22. "A" worked five days on overhauling an old car. Then "B" worked four days to finish the job. After the sale of the car, the net profit was $243. They wanted to divide the profit on the basis of time spent by each. A's share of the profit was
    A. $108
    B. $135
    C. $127
    D. $143

    22._____

Questions 23-26

DIRECTIONS: Each of the following questions contains four sentences. Select the sentence in each question that is best with respect to grammar and good usage.

23. A. One of us have to make the reply before tomorrow.
    B. Making the reply before tomorrow will have to be done by one of us.
    C. One of us has to reply before tomorrow.
    D. Anyone has to reply before tomorrow.

    23._____

24. A. There is several ways to organize a good report.
    B. Several ways exist in organizing a good report.
    C. To organize a good report, several ways exist.
    D. There are several ways to organize a good report.

    24._____

25. A. All employees whose record of service ranged between 51 down to 40 years were retired.
    B. All employees who had served from 40 to 51 years were retired.
    C. All employees serving 40 to 51 years were retired.
    D. Those retired were employees serving 40 to 51 years.

    25._____

26. A. Of all the employees, he spends the most time at the office.
    B. He spends more time at the office than that of his employees.
    C. His working hours are longer than or equal to those of other employees.
    D. He devotes as much, if not more, time to his work than the rest of the employees.

    26._____

Question 27 is based on the following paragraph:

Certain inmate types are generally found in prisons. These types are called gorillas, toughs, hipsters and merchants. Gorillas deliberately use violence to intimidate fearful inmates into providing favors. Toughs are swift to explode into violence against prisoners, because of real or imagined insults. Exploitation of others is not their major goal. Hipsters are bullies who choose victims with caution in order to win acceptance among inmates by demonstrating physical bravery. Their bravery, however, is false. Merchants exploit other inmates through manipulation in sharp trading of goods stolen from prison supplies or in trickery in gambling.

27. Martins frequently beats up Smith and Brooks. Smith and Brooks provide Martins with extra cigarettes and coffee. Martins is a
    A. tough
    B. gorilla
    C. merchant
    D. hipster

Questions 28 through 30 are based on the following description of the duties of the Court Officer:

Throughout the session of the court, the officer must see that proper order and decorum are maintained in the courtroom. Above all else, silence must be constantly observed, and every possible distraction must be eliminated so as not to delay the most efficient functioning of the court.
　　The officer must carry out such duties as may be required by the court and clerk. Examples of such duties are directing witnesses to the witness stand and assisting the Court Clerk and counsel in the handling of exhibits. At times, the officer must act as a messenger in procuring any books from the court library that are required by the attorneys and ordered by the Court Clerk.
　　The enforcement of the rules of the court requires courteous behavior on the part of the Court Officer, although firmness and strictness are necessary when the occasion requires such an attitude.

28. Testimony has been given, the witnesses have been cross-examined and the attorneys have given their summations. Now the judge is charging the jury. A Court Officer has been stationed outside the courtroom door to prevent anyone from entering during the charge. The City Council President arrives, accompanied by a woman, and attempts to enter the courtroom. The Court Officer should
    A. apologize and explain why they cannot be permitted to enter
    B. permit the man to enter, since he is the City Council President, but exclude the woman
    C. permit them to enter because surely the judge would make an exception for such important people
    D. send a note to the judge to ask whether they may be permitted to enter

29. A witness who is waiting to be called to the stand appears to be very nervous. He wiggles and squirms, stands and stretches, looks over his shoulder at the courtroom door and waves to spectators. The officer should
    A. tell the witness to leave the courtroom at once
    B. handcuff the witness
    C. ask the witness to please sit still and try to restrain himself
    D. suggest to the judge that he call this witness next

29._____

30. During the course of cross-examination, a defendant frequently refers to a book that she claims has had a great influence on her life and that she claims justifies her behavior in the crime for which she is charged. In the jury box, two jurors begin a lively discussion of whether the defendant is quoting accurately. The best action for the Court Officer is to
    A. ask the Court Clerk for permission to go to the library to get the book
    B. send a messenger to get the book
    C. assure the jurors that the book is being accurately quoted and that only the interpretation is in question
    D. remind the jurors that they are not to converse in the courtroom

30._____

31. "Ideally, a correctional system should include several types of institutions to provide different degrees of custody."
    On the basis of this statement, one could most reasonably say that
    A. as the number of institutions in a correctional system increases, the efficiency of the system increases
    B. the difference in degree of custody for the inmate depends on the types of institutions in a correctional system
    C. the greater the variety of institutions, the stricter the degree of custody that can be maintained
    D. the same type of correctional institution is not desirable for the custody of all prisoners

31._____

32. "The enforced idleness of a large percentage of adult men and women in our prisons is one of the direct causes of the tensions that burst forth in riot and disorder."
    On the basis of this statement, a good reason why inmates should perform daily work of some kind is that
    A. better morale and discipline can be maintained when inmates are kept busy
    B. daily work is an effective way of punishing inmates for the crimes they have committed
    C. law-abiding citizens must work therefore labor should also be required of inmates
    D. products of inmates' labor will in part pay the cost of their maintenance

32._____

33. "With industry invading rural areas, the use of the automobile, and the speed of modern communications and transportation, the problems of neglect and delinquency are no longer peculiar to cities but are an established feature of everyday life."
This statement implies most directly that
    A. delinquents are moving from cities to rural areas
    B. delinquency and neglect are found in rural areas
    C. delinquency is not as much of a problem in rural areas as in cities
    D. rural areas now surpass cities in industry

33._____

34. "Young men from minority groups, if unable to find employment, become discouraged and hopeless because of their economic position and may finally resort to any means of supplying their wants."
The most reasonable of the following conclusions that may be drawn from this statement only is that
    A. discouragement sometimes leads to crime
    B. in general, young men from minority groups are criminals
    C. unemployment turns young men from crime
    D. young men from minority groups are seldom employed

34._____

35. "To prevent crime, we must deal with the possible criminals long before they reach the prison. Our aim should be not merely to reform the lawbreakers but to strike at the roots of crime: neglectful parents, bad companions, unsatisfactory homes, selfishness, disregard for the rights of others and bad social conditions."
The above statement recommends
    A. abolition of prisons
    B. better reformatories
    C. compulsory education
    D. general social reform

35._____

36. "There is evidence that shows that comic books which glorify the criminal and criminal acts have a distinct influence in producing young criminals."
According to this statement
    A. comic books affect the development of criminal careers
    B. comic books specialize in reporting criminal acts
    C. young criminals read comic books exclusively
    D. young criminals should not be permitted to read comic books

36._____

37. A study shows that juvenile delinquents are equal in intelligence to but three school grades behind juvenile nondelinquents. On the basis of this information only, it is most reasonable to say that
    A. a delinquent usually progresses to the educational limit set by intelligence
    B. educational achievement depends on intelligence only
    C. educational achievement is closely associated with delinquency
    D. lack of intelligence is closely associated with delinquency

37._____

38. "Prevention of crime is of greater value to the community than the punishment of crime."
    If this statement is accepted as true, greatest emphasis should be placed on
    A. execution
    B. medication
    C. imprisonment
    D. rehabilitation

39. A Court Assistant being instructed in his duties was told by the Court Clerk, "experience is the best teacher."
    The one of the following that most nearly expresses the meaning of this quotation is:
    A. A good teacher will make a hard job look easy
    B. Bad experience does more harm than good
    C. Lack of experience will make an easy job hard
    D. The best way to learn to do a thing is by doing it

40. "Once the purposes or goals of an organization have been determined, they must be communicated to subordinate levels of supervisory staff."
    On the basis of this quotation, the most accurate statement is that
    A. supervisory personnel should participate in the formulation of the goals of an organization
    B. the structure of an organization should be considered in determining the organization's goals
    C. the goals that have been established for the different levels of an organization should be reviewed regularly
    D. information about the goals of an organization should be distributed to supervisory personnel

41. "Close examination of traffic accident statistics reveals that traffic accidents are frequently the result of violations of traffic laws—and usually the violations are the result of illegal and dangerous driving behavior, rather than the result of mechanical defects or poor road conditions."
    According to this statement, the majority of dangerous traffic violations are cause by
    A. poor driving
    B. bad roads
    C. unsafe cars
    D. unwise traffic laws

Questions 42 through 44 are based on the following paragraph:

The supervisor gains the respect of his staff members and increases his influence over them by controlling his temper and avoiding criticizing anyone publicly. When a mistake is made, the good supervisor will talk it over with the employee quietly and privately. The supervisor listens to the employee's story, suggests a better way to do the job, and offers help so the mistake won't happen again. Before closing the discussion, the supervisor should try to find something good to say about other aspects of the employee's work. Some praise and appreciation, along with instruction, is likely to encourage an employee to improve in those areas where he is weakest.

42. A good title that would show the meaning of this entire paragraph would be:
    A. How to Correct Employee Errors
    B. How to Praise Employees
    C. Mistakes are Preventable
    D. The Weak Employee

43. According to the preceding paragraph, the work of an employee who has made a mistake is more likely to improve if the supervisor
    A. avoids criticizing him
    B. gives him a chance to suggest a better way of doing the work
    C. listens to the employee's excuses to see if he's right
    D. praises good work at the same time he corrects the mistake

44. When a supervisor needs to correct an employee's mistake, it is important that he
    A. allow some time to go by after the mistake has been made
    B. do so when other employees are not present
    C. show his influence by his tone of voice
    D. tell other employees to avoid the same mistake

45. "Determination of total, or even partial, guilt and responsibility as viewed by law cannot be made solely on the basis of a consideration of the external factors of the case, but rather should be made mainly in the light of the individual defendant's history and development."
    The above statement reflects a philosophy of law that requires that
    A. the punishment fit the crime
    B. the individual, rather than the crime, be considered first
    C. motivations behind a crime are relatively unimportant
    D. the individual's knowledge of right and wrong be the sole determinant of guilt

46. A traffic regulation says, "No driver shall enter an intersection unless there is sufficient unobstructed space beyond the intersection to accommodate the vehicle he or she is operating, not withstanding any traffic-control signal indication to the contrary."
This regulation means that:
    A. a driver should not go through an intersection if there are no parking spaces available on the next block
    B. a driver should not enter an intersection when the traffic light is red
    C. a driver should not enter an intersection if traffic ahead is so badly backed up that he or she would not be able to go ahead and would block the intersection
    D. a driver should ignore traffic signals completely whenever there are obstructions in the road ahead

46._____

Questions 47 through 51 are based on the following passage:

A large proportion of people behind bars are not convicted criminals, but people who have been arrested and are being held until their trial in court. Experts have often pointed out that this detention system does not operate fairly. For instance, a person who can afford to pay bail usually will not get locked up.

The theory of the bail system is that the person will make sure to show up in court when he or she is supposed to; otherwise, bail will be forfeited—the person will lose the money that was put up. Sometimes a person who can show that he or she is a stable citizen with a job and a family will be released on "personal recognizance" (without bail). The result is that the well-to-do, the employed and the family men can often avoid the detention system. The people who do wind up in detention tend to be the poor, the unemployed, the single and the young.

47. People who are put behind bars
    A. are almost always dangerous criminals
    B. include many innocent people who have been arrested by mistake
    C. are often people who have been arrested but have not yet come to trial
    D. are all poor people who tend to be young and single

47._____

48. The passage says that the detention system works unfairly against people who are
    A. rich
    B. old
    C. married
    D. unemployed

48._____

49. The passage uses the expression "bail will be forfeited." Even if you had not seen the word *forfeit* before, you could figure out from the way it is used that forfeiting probably means _____ something.
    A. losing track of
    B. finding
    C. giving up
    D. avoiding

49._____

50. When someone is released on personal recognizance, this means that
    A. the judge knows that the person is innocent
    B. he or she does not have to show up for a trial
    C. he or she has a record of previous convictions
    D. he or she does not have to pay bail

    50._____

51. Suppose that two men were booked on the same charge at the same time and that the same bail was set for both of them. One man was able to put up bail and was released. The second man was not able to put up bail and was held in detention. The writer of the passage would most likely feel that this result is
    A. unfair, because it does not have any relationship to guilt or innocence
    B. unfair, because the first man deserves severe punishment
    C. fair, because the first man is obviously innocent
    D. fair, because the law should be tougher on the poor people than on the rich

    51._____

Questions 52 through 55 are based on the following passage:

The Court Officer has important functions in connection with control of the jury. He or she must confirm that every juror has the proper place in the box and must be constantly on watch to prevent any juror from leaving the jury box while the trial is in progress. Should a juror decide to leave the box while the case is going on, the Court Officer must first inform the judge of the juror's desire to determine whether the judge will grant or refuse the juror's wish. If the judge approves, the trial is stopped and the Court Officer is instructed to accompany the juror while he or she is out of the jury box.

In order to prevent any stoppage or mistrial, the Court Officer must not allow the juror to get out of the range of sight or hearing. The officer must always bear in mind that the juror should be returned as quickly as possible, without any unnecessary delay. The juror must not enter into any conversation with anybody or read any matter that he or she may have or that may be given by another person.

The Court Officer must be particularly careful when placed in charge of a jury that has retired to deliberate. The Court Officer must conduct the jury to the jury room and see to it that no juror talks with anyone on the way. If a juror does talk with someone, the event may afford grounds for a mistrial.

52. A juror has requested and received permission to go to the men's room. As he approaches the door, he takes out a sports magazine he has brought from home as "bathroom literature." The Court Officer should
    A. permit the juror to read the magazine
    B. check the magazine for papers that might be hidden between the pages, then let the juror read it
    C. offer the juror something of his own to read, something that he knows will not influence the juror in any way
    D. tell the juror that reading in the men's room is not permitted

    52._____

53. While leading a jury from the courtroom to the jury room, a Court Officer notices a person leaning against a corridor wall making active hand motions as a juror stares intently. The *first* thing for a Court Officer to do is
    A. tell the juror to look straight ahead and keep walking
    B. step between the juror and the person so as to interrupt the juror's line of vision
    C. ask the juror what he is looking at
    D. call a police officer to arrest the person with the active hands

53._____

54. If the Court Officer ascertains that a message has been transmitted by an outside person to a juror, it would be best for the Court Officer to
    A. keep this information secret
    B. ask the juror what the message was about
    C. deliver the juror to the jury room, then discuss the matter with the Court Clerk
    D. accompany the juror to the judge and tell the judge exactly what the Court Officer observed

54._____

55. During the course of testimony, a juror begins to cough uncontrollably. The coughing is loud and distressing. The Court Officer should
    A. summon a doctor at once
    B. lead the juror from the courtroom as quickly and quietly as possible
    C. bring the juror a glass of water
    D. ask the judge what to do

55._____

KEY (CORRECT ANSWERS)

1. C	11. A	21. C	31. D	41. A	51. A
2. B	12. D	22. B	32. A	42. A	52. D
3. B	13. C	23. C	33. B	43. D	53. A
4. C	14. C	24. D	34. A	44. B	54. B
5. C	15. D	25. B	35. D	45. B	55. B
6. A	16. C	26. A	36. A	46. C	
7. B	17. C	27. B	37. C	47. C	
8. C	18. A	28. A	38. D	48. D	
9. A	19. D	29. C	39. D	49. C	
10. A	20. C	30. D	40. D	50. D	

EXAMINATION SECTION
TEST 1

DIRECTIONS: Each question or incomplete statement is followed by several suggested answers or completions. Select the one that BEST answers the question or completes the statement. *PRINT THE LETTER OF THE CORRECT ANSWER IN THE SPACE AT THE RIGHT.*

Questions 1-4.

DIRECTIONS: Questions 1 through 4 are based on the picture entitled *Contents of a Woman's Handbag*. Assume that all of the contents are shown in the picture.

<u>CONTENTS OF A WOMAN'S HANDBAG</u>

1. Where does Gladys Constantine live?

   A. Chalmers Street in Manhattan
   B. Summer Street in Manhattan
   C. Summer Street in Brooklyn
   D. Chalmers Street in Brooklyn

2. How many keys were in the handbag?

   A. 2   B. 3   C. 4   D. 5

3. How much money was in the handbag? _____ dollar(s).

   A. Exactly five   B. More than five
   C. Exactly ten   D. Less than one

4. The sales slip found in the handbag shows the purchase of which of the following?

   A. The handbag   B. Lipstick
   C. Tissues   D. Prescription medicine

Questions 5-8.

DIRECTIONS: Questions 5 through 8 are based on the floor plan below.

FLOOR PLAN

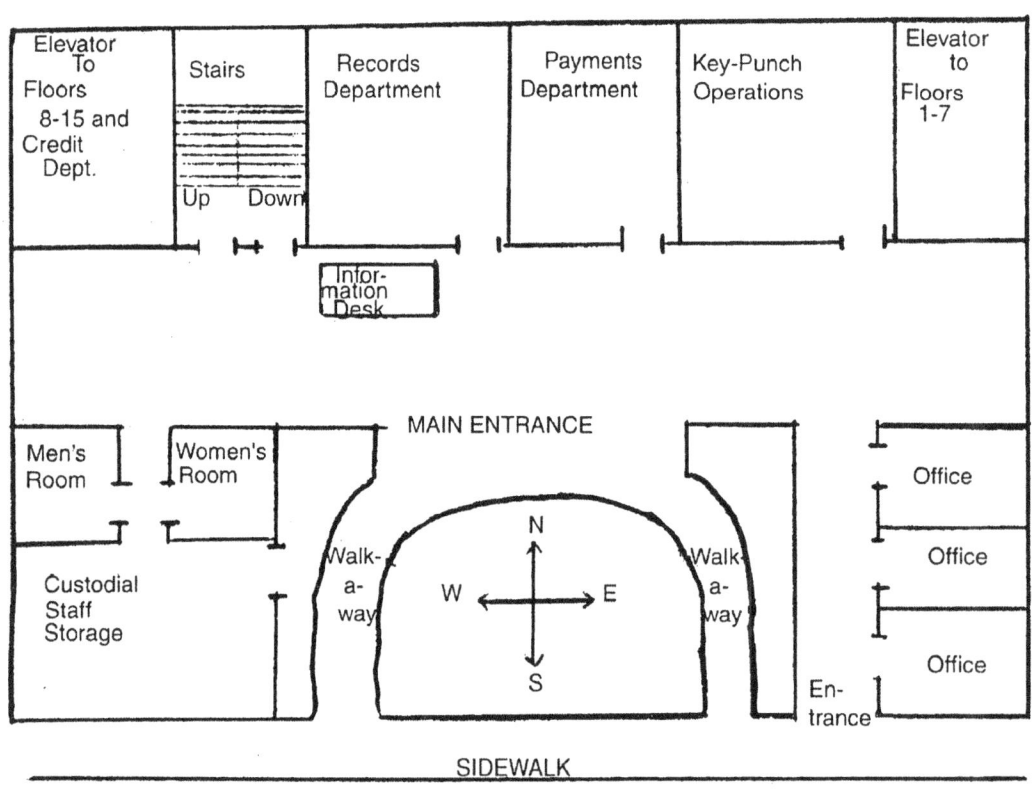

5. A special officer (security officer) on duty at the main entrance must be aware of other outside entrances to his area of the building. These unguarded entrances are usually kept locked, but they are important in case of fire or other emergency.
   Besides the main entrance, how many OTHER entrances shown on the floor plan directly face Forty-ninth Street?
   _____ other entrances.

   A. No B. One C. Two D. Three

6. A person who arrives at the main entrance and asks to be directed to the Credit Department SHOULD be told to

   A. take the elevator on the left
   B. take the elevator on the right
   C. go to a different entrance
   D. go up the stairs on the left

7. On the east side of the entrance can be found

   A. a storage room   B. offices
   C. toilets   D. stairs

8. The space DIRECTLY BEHIND the Information Desk in the floor plan is occupied by

   A. up and down stairs   B. key punch operations
   C. toilets   D. the records department

Questions 9-12.

DIRECTIONS: Answer Questions 9 to 12 on the basis of the information given in the passage below.

The public often believes that the main job of a uniformed officer is to enforce laws by simply arresting people. In reality, however, many of the situations that an officer deals with do not call for the use of his arrest power. In the first place, an officer spends much of his time <u>preventing</u> crimes from happening, by spotting potential violations or suspicious behavior and taking action to prevent illegal acts. In the second place, many of the situations in which officers are called on for assistance involve elements like personal arguments, husband-wife quarrels, noisy juveniles, or mentally disturbed persons. The majority of these problems do not result in arrests and convictions, and often they do not even involve illegal behavior. In the third place, even in situations where there seems to be good reason to make an arrest, an officer may have to exercise very good judgment. There are times when making an arrest too soon could touch off a riot, or could result in the detention of a minor offender while major offenders escaped, or could cut short the gathering of necessary on-the-scene evidence.

9. The above passage IMPLIES that most citizens

   A. will start to riot if they see an arrest being made
   B. appreciate the work that law enforcement officers do
   C. do not realize that making arrests is only a small part of law enforcement
   D. never call for assistance unless they are involved in a personal argument or a husband-wife quarrel

10. According to the passage, one way in which law enforcement officers can prevent crimes from happening is by

   A. arresting suspicious characters
   B. letting minor offenders go free
   C. taking action on potential violations
   D. refusing to get involved in husband-wife fights

11. According to the passage, which of the following statements is NOT true of situations involving mentally disturbed persons?

   A. It is a waste of time to call on law enforcement officers for assistance in such situations.
   B. Such situations may not involve illegal behavior
   C. Such situations often do not result in arrests.
   D. Citizens often turn to law enforcement officers for help in such situations.

12. The last sentence in the passage mentions *detention of minor offenders.*
   Of the following, which BEST explains the meaning of the word *detention* as used here?

   A. Sentencing someone
   B. Indicting someone
   C. Calling someone before a grand jury
   D. Arresting someone

Questions 13-28.

DIRECTIONS: In answering Questions 13 through 28, assume that *you* means a special officer (security officer) on duty. Your basic responsibilities are safeguarding people and property and maintaining order in the area to which you are assigned. You are in uniform, and you are not armed. You keep in touch with your supervisory station either by telephone or by a two-way radio (walkie-talkie).

13. It is a general rule that if the security alarm goes off showing that someone has made an unlawful entrance into a building, no officer responsible for security shall proceed to investigate alone. Each officer must be accompanied by at least one other officer.
   Of the following, which is the MOST probable reason for this rule?

   A. It is dangerous for an officer to investigate such a situation alone.
   B. The intruder might try to bribe an officer to let him go.
   C. One officer may be inexperienced and needs an experienced partner.
   D. Two officers are better than one officer in writing a report of the investigation.

14. You are on weekend duty on the main floor of a public building. The building is closed to the public on weekends, but some employees are sometimes asked to work weekends. You have been instructed to use cautious good judgment in opening the door for such persons.
   Of the following, which one MOST clearly shows the poorest judgment?

A. Admitting an employee who is personally known to you without asking to see any identification except the permit slip signed by the employee's supervisor
B. Refusing to admit someone whom you do not recognize but who claims left his identification at home
C. Admitting to the building only those who can give a detailed description of their weekend work duties
D. Leaving the entrance door locked for a while to make regulation security checks of other areas in the building with the result that no one can either enter or leave during these periods

15. You are on duty at a public building. An office employee tells you that she left her purse in her desk when she went out to lunch, and she has just discovered that it is gone. She has been back from lunch for half an hour and has not left her desk during this period. What should you do FIRST?

    A. Warn all security personnel to stop any suspicious-looking person who is seen with a purse
    B. Ask for a description of the purse
    C. Call the Lost and Found and ask if a purse has been turned in
    D. Obtain statements from any employees who were in the office during the lunch hour

16. You are patrolling your assigned area in a public building. You hear a sudden crash and the sound of running footsteps. You investigate and find that someone has forced open a locked entrance to the building. What is the FIRST thing you should do?

    A. Close the door and try to fix the lock so that no one else can get in
    B. Use your two-way radio to report the emergency and summon help
    C. Chase after the person whose running footsteps you heard
    D. Go immediately to your base office and make out a brief written report

17. You and another special officer (security officer) are on duty in the main waiting area at a welfare center. A caseworker calls both of you over and whispers that one of the clients, Richard Roe, may be carrying a gun. Of the following, what is the BEST action for both of you to take?

    A. You should approach the man, one on each side, and one of you should say loudly and clearly, "Richard Roe, you are under arrest."
    B. Both of you should ask the man to go with you to a private room, and then find out if he is carrying a gun
    C. Both of you should grab him, handcuff him, and take him to the nearest precinct station house
    D. Both of you should watch him carefully but not do anything unless he actually pulls a gun

18. You are on duty at a welfare center. You are told that a caseworker is being threatened by a man with a knife. You go immediately to the scene, and you find the caseworker lying on the floor with blood spurting from a wound in his arm. You do not know who the attacker is. What should you do FIRST?

    A. Ask the caseworker for a description of the attacker so that you can set out in pursuit and try to catch him
    B. Take down the names and addresses of any witnesses to the incident

C. Give first aid to the caseworker, if you can, and immediately call for an ambulance
D. Search the people standing around in the room for the knife

19. As a special officer (security officer), you have been patrolling a special section of a hospital building for a week. Smoking is not allowed in this section because the oxygen tanks in use here could easily explode. However, you have observed that some employees sneak into the linen-supply room in this section in order to smoke without anybody seeing them.
Of the following, which is the BEST way for you to deal with this situation?

    A. Whenever you catch anyone smoking, call his supervisor immediately
    B. Request the Building Superintendent to put a padlock on the door of the linen-supply room
    C. Ignore the smoking because you do not want to get a reputation for interfering in the private affairs of other employees
    D. Report the situation to your supervisor and follow his instructions

20. You are on duty at a hospital. You have been assigned to guard the main door, and you are responsible for remaining at your post until relieved. On one of the wards for which you are not responsible, there is a patient who was wounded in a street fight. This patient is under arrest for killing another man in this fight, and he is supposed to be under round-the-clock police guard. A nurse tells you that one of the police officers assigned to guard the patient has suddenly taken ill and has to periodically leave his post to go to the washroom. The nurse is worried because she thinks the patient might try to escape.
Of the following, which is the BEST action for you to take?

    A. Tell the nurse to call you whenever the police officer leaves his post so that you can keep an eye on the patient while the officer is gone
    B. Assume that the police officer probably knows his job, and that there is no reason for you to worry
    C. Alert your supervisor to the nurse's report
    D. Warn the police officer that the nurse has been talking about him

21. You are on night duty at a hospital where you are responsible for patrolling a large section of the main building. Your supervisor tells you that there have been several nighttime thefts from a supply room in your section and asks you to be especially alert for suspicious activity near this supply room.
Of the following, which is the MOST reasonable way to carry out your supervisor's direction?

    A. Check the supply room regularly at half-hour intervals
    B. Make frequent checks of the supply room at irregular intervals
    C. Station yourself by the door of the supply room and stay at this post all night
    D. Find a hidden spot from which you can watch the supply room and stay there all night

22. You are on duty at a vehicle entrance to a hospital. Parking space on the hospital grounds is strictly limited, and no one is ever allowed to park there unless they have an official parking permit. You have just stopped a driver who does not have a parking permit, but he explains that
he is a doctor and he has a patient in the hospital. What should you do?

A. Let him park since he has explained that he is a doctor
B. Ask in a friendly way, *"Can I check your identification?"*
C. Call the Information Desk to make sure there is such a patient in the hospital
D. Tell the driver politely but firmly that he will have to park somewhere else

23. You are on duty at a public building. A man was just mugged on a stairway. The mugger took the man's wallet and started to run down the stairs but tripped and fell. Now the mugger is lying unconscious at the bottom of the stairs and bleeding from the mouth.
The FIRST thing you should do is to

    A. search him to see if he is carrying any other stolen property
    B. pick him up and carry him away from the stairs
    C. try and revive him for questioning
    D. put in a call for an ambulance and police assistance

24. After someone breaks into an employee's locker at a public building, you interview the employee to determine what is missing from the locker. The employee becomes hysterical and asks why you are *wasting time with all these questions* instead of going after the thief.
The MOST reasonable thing for you to do is

    A. tell the employee that it is very important to have an accurate description of the missing articles
    B. quietly tell the employee to calm down and stop interfering with your work
    C. explain to the employee that you are only doing what you were told to do and that you don't make the rules
    D. assure the employee that there are a lot of people working on the case and that someone else is probably arresting the thief right now

25. You are on duty at a public building. An employee reports that a man has just held her up and taken her money. The employee says that the man was about 25 years old, with short blond hair and a pale complexion and was wearing blue jeans.
Of the following additional facts, which one would probably be MOST valuable to officers searching the building for the suspect?

    A. The man was wearing dark glasses.
    B. He had on a green jacket.
    C. He was about 5 feet 8 inches tall.
    D. His hands and fingernails were very dirty.

26. When the fire alarm goes off, it is your job as a special officer (security officer) to see that all employees leave the building quickly by the correct exits. A fire alarm has just sounded, and you are checking the offices on one of the floors. A supervisor in one office tells you, *"This is probably just another fire drill. I've sent my office staff out, but I don't want to stop my own work."*
What should you do?

    A. Insist politely but firmly that the supervisor must obey the fire rules.
    B. Tell the supervisor that it is all right this time but that the rules must be followed in the future.
    C. Tell the supervisor that he is under arrest.
    D. Allow the supervisor to do as he sees fit since he is in charge of his own office.

27. You are on duty on the main floor of a public building. You have been informed that a briefcase has just been stolen from an office on the tenth floor. You see a man getting off the elevator with a briefcase that matches the description of the one that was stolen.
What is the FIRST action you should take?

   A. Arrest the man and take him to the nearest public station
   B. Stop the man and say politely that you want to take a look at the briefcase
   C. Take the briefcase from the man and tell him that he cannot have it back unless he can prove that it is his
   D. Do not stop the man but note down his description and the exact time he got off the elevator

28. You are on duty at a welfare center. You have been told that two clients are arguing with a caseworker and making loud threats. You go to the scene, but the caseworker tells you that everything is now under control. The two clients, who are both mean-looking characters, are still there but seem to be acting normally.
What SHOULD you do?

   A. Apologize for having made a mistake and go away.
   B. Arrest the two men for having caused a disturbance.
   C. Insist on standing by until the interview is over, then escort the two men from the building.
   D. Leave the immediate scene but watch for any further developments.

29. You are on duty at a welfare center. A client comes up to you and says that two men just threatened him with a knife and made him give them his money. The client has alcohol on his breath and he is shabbily dressed. He points out the two men he says took the money.
Of the following, which is the BEST action to take?

   A. Arrest the two men on the client's complaint.
   B. Ignore the client's complaint since he doesn't look as if he could have had any money.
   C. Suggest to the client that he may be imagining things.
   D. Investigate and find out what happened.

Questions 30-35.

DIRECTIONS: Answer Questions 30 through 35 on the basis of the information given in the passage below. Assume that all questions refer to the same state described in the passage.

The courts and the police consider an "offense" as any conduct that is punishable by a fine or imprisonment. Such offenses include many kinds of acts - from behavior that is merely annoying, like throwing a noisy party that keeps everyone awake, all the way up to violent acts like murder. The law classifies offenses according to the penalties that are provided for them. In one state, minor offenses are called "violations." A violation is punishable by a fine of not more than $250 or imprisonment of not more than. 15 days, or both. The annoying behavior mentioned above is an example of a violation. More serious offenses are classified as "crimes." Crimes are classified by the kind of penalty that is provided. A "misdemeanor" is a crime that is punishable by a fine of not more than $1,000 or by imprisonment of not more than one year, or both. Examples of misdemeanors include stealing something with a value *of $100 or less, turning in a false alarm, or illegally possessing less than 1/8 of an ounce of a dangerous drug. A "felony" is a criminal offense punishable by imprisonment of more than one year. Murder is clearly a felony.*

30. According to the above passage, any act that is punishable by imprisonment or by a fine is called a(n)

    A. offense B. violation C. crime D. felony

31. According to the above passage, which of the following is classified as a crime?

    A. Offense punishable by 15 days imprisonment
    B. Minor offense
    C. Violation
    D. Misdemeanor

32. According to the above passage, if a person guilty of burglary can receive a prison sentence of 7 years or more, burglary would be classified as a

    A. violation
    B. misdemeanor
    C. felony
    D. violent act

33. According to the above passage, two offenses that would BOTH be classified as misdemeanors are

    A. making unreasonable noise and stealing a $90 bicycle
    B. stealing a $75 radio and possessing 1/16 of an ounce of heroin
    C. holding up a bank and possessing 1/4 of a pound of marijuana
    D. falsely reporting a fire and illegally double-parking

34. The above passage says that offenses are classified according to the penalties provided for them.
    On the basis of clues in the passage, who probably decides what the maximum penalties should be for the different kinds of offenses?

    A. The State lawmakers
    B. The City police
    C. The Mayor
    D. Officials in Washington, B.C.

35. Of the following, which BEST describes the subject matter of the passage?

    A. How society deals with criminals
    B. How offenses are classified
    C. Three types of criminal behavior
    D. The police approach to offenders

KEY (CORRECT ANSWERS)

1. C
2. C
3. B
4. D
5. B

6. A
7. B
8. D
9. C
10. C

11. A
12. D
13. A
14. C
15. B

16. B
17. B
18. C
19. D
20. C

21. B
22. D
23. D
24. A
25. C

26. A
27. B
28. D
29. D
30. A

31. D
32. C
33. B
34. A
35. B

TEST 2

DIRECTIONS: Each question or incomplete statement is followed by several suggested answers or completions. Select the one that BEST answers the question or completes the statement. *PRINT THE LETTER OF THE CORRECT ANSWER IN THE SPACE AT THE RIGHT.*

Questions 1-5.

DIRECTIONS: Questions 1 through 5 are based on the drawing below showing a view of a waiting area in a public building.

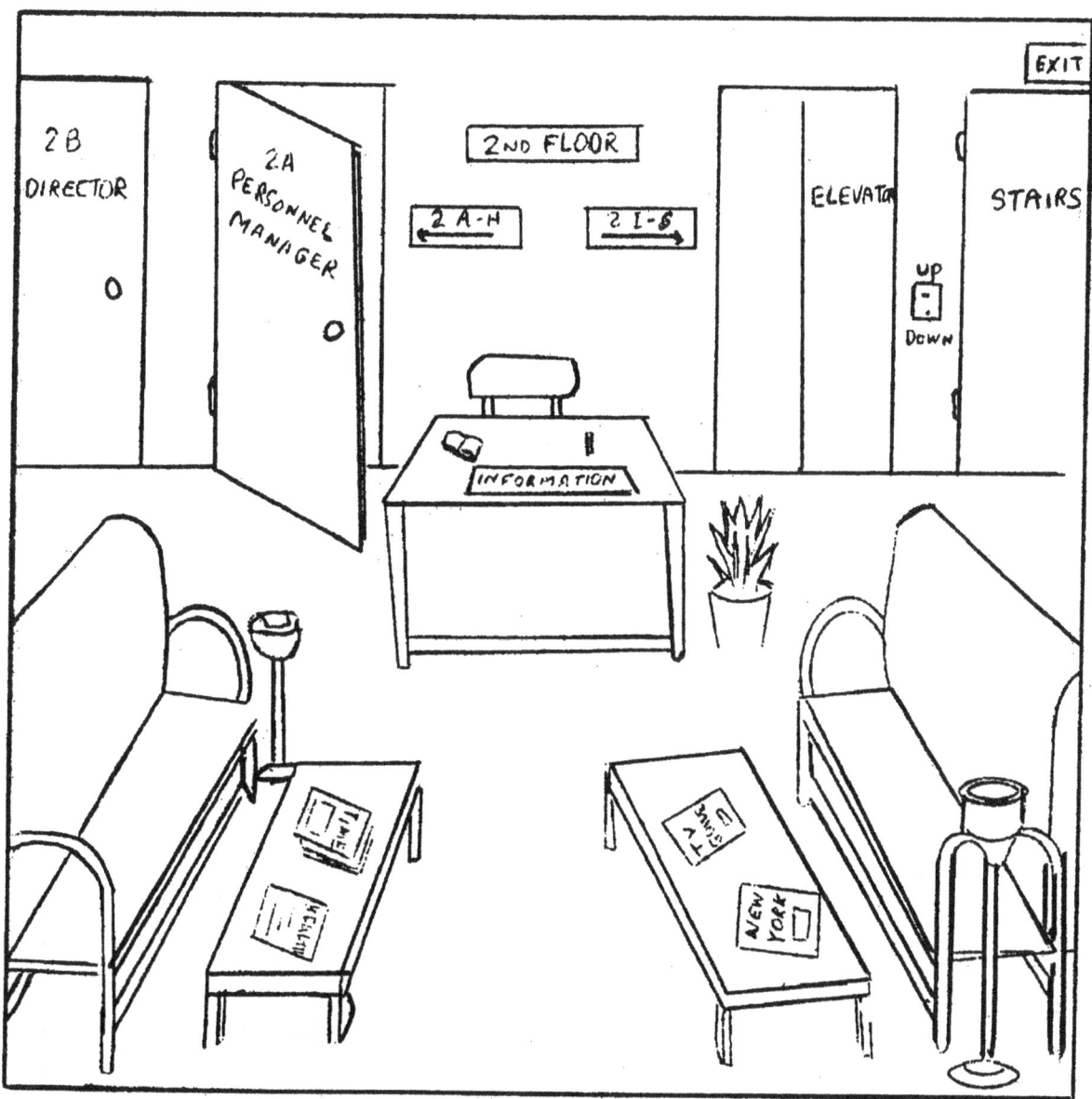

1. A desk is shown in the drawing. Which of the following is on the desk? A(n) 1._____

    A. plant   B. telephone
    C. In-Out file   D. *Information* sign

45

2. On which floor is the waiting area? 2.___

   A. Basement   B. Main floor
   C. Second floor   D. Third floor

3. The door IMMEDIATELY TO THE RIGHT of the desk is a(n) 3.___

   A. door to the Personnel Office
   B. elevator door
   C. door to another corridor
   D. door to the stairs

4. Among the magazines on the tables in the waiting area are 4.___

   A. TIME and NEWSWEEK
   B. READER'S DIGEST and T.V. GUIDE
   C. NEW YORK and READER'S DIGEST
   D. TIME and T.V. GUIDE

5. One door is partly open. This is the door to 5.___

   A. the Director's office
   B. the Personnel Manager's office
   C. the stairs
   D. an unmarked office

Questions 6-9.

DIRECTIONS: Questions 6 through 9 are based on the drawing below showing the contents of a male suspect's pockets.

CONTENTS OF A MALE SUSPECT'S POCKETS

6. The suspect had a slip in his pockets showing an appointment at an out-patient clinic on 6.____

   A. February 9, 2013   B. September 2, 2013
   C. February 19, 2013   D. September 12, 2013

7. The MP3 player that was found on the suspect was made by 7.____

   A. RCA   B. GE   C. Sony   D. Zenith

8. The coins found in the suspect's pockets have a TOTAL value of 8.____

   A. 56¢   B. 77¢   C. $1.05   D. $1.26

9. All except one of the following were found in the suspect's pockets. 9.____
   Which was NOT found? A

   A. ticket stub   B. comb
   C. subway fare   D. pen

Questions 10-18

DIRECTIONS: In answering Questions 10 through 18, assume that *you* means a special officer (security officer) on duty. Your basic responsibilities are safeguarding people and property and maintaining order in the area to which you are assigned. You are in uniform, and you are not armed. You keep in touch with your supervisory station either by telephone or by a two-way radio (a walkie-talkie).

10. You are on duty at a center run by the Department of Social Services. Two teenaged 10.____
    boys are on their way out of the center. As they go past you, they look at you and laugh, and one makes a remark to you in Spanish. You do not understand Spanish, but you suspect it was a nasty remark.
    What SHOULD you do?

    A. Give the boys a lecture about showing respect for a uniform.
    B. Tell the boys that they had better stay away from the center from now on.
    C. Call for an interpreter and insist that the boy repeat the remark to the interpreter.
    D. Let the boys go on their way since they have done nothing requiring your intervention.

11. You are on duty at a shelter run by the Department of Social Services. You know that 11.____
    many of the shelter clients have drinking problems, drug problems, or mental health problems. You get a call for assistance from a caseworker who says a fight has broken out. When you arrive on the scene, you see that about a dozen clients are engaged in a free-for-all and that two or three of them have pulled knives.
    The BEST course of action is to

    A. call for additional assistance and order all bystanders away from the area
    B. jump into the center of the fighting group and try to separate the fighters
    C. pick up a heavy object and start swinging at anybody who has a knife
    D. try to find out what clients started the fight and place them under arrest

12. You have been assigned to duty at a children's shelter run by the Department of Social Services. The children range in age from 6 to 15, and many of them are at the shelter because they have no homes to go to.
    Of the following, which is the BEST attitude for you to take in dealing with these youngsters?

    A. Assume that they admire and respect anyone in uniform and that they will not usually give you much trouble
    B. Assume that they fear and distrust anyone in uniform and that they are going to give you a hard time unless you act tough
    C. Expect that many of them are going to become juvenile delinquents because of their bad backgrounds and that you should be suspicious of everything they do
    D. Expect that many of them may be emotionally upset and that you should be alert for unusual behavior

13. You are on duty outside the emergency room of a hospital. You notice that an old man has been sitting on a bench outside the room for a long time. He arrived alone, and he has not spoken to anyone at all.
    What SHOULD you do?

    A. Pay no attention to him since he is not bothering anyone.
    B. Tell him to leave since he does not seem to have any business there.
    C. Ask him if you can help him in any way.
    D. Do not speak to him, but keep an eye on him.

14. You are patrolling a section of a public building. An elderly woman carrying a heavy shopping bag asks you if you would watch the shopping bag for her while she keeps an appointment in the building.
    What SHOULD you do?

    A. Watch the shopping bag for her since her appointment probably will not take long.
    B. Refuse her request, explaining that your duties keep you on the move.
    C. Agree to her request just to be polite, but then continue your patrol after the woman is out of sight.
    D. Find a bystander who will agree to watch the shopping bag for her.

15. You are on duty at a public building. It is nearly 6:00 P.M., and most employees have left for the day.
    You see two well-dressed men carrying an office calculating machine out of the building. You SHOULD

    A. stop them and ask for an explanation
    B. follow them to see where they are going
    C. order them to put down the machine and leave the building immediately
    D. take no action since they do not look like burglars

16. You are on duty patrolling a public building. You have just tripped on the stairs and turned your ankle. The ankle hurts and is starting to swell.
    What is the BEST thing to do?

A. Take a taxi to a hospital emergency room, and from there have a hospital employee call your supervisor to explain the situation.
B. First try soaking your foot in cold water for half an hour, then go off duty if you really cannot walk at all.
C. Report the situation to your supervisor, explaining that you need prompt medical attention for your ankle.
D. Find a place where you can sit until you are due to go off duty, then have a doctor look at your ankle.

17. One of your duties as a special officer (security officer) on night patrol in a public building is to check the washrooms to see that the taps are turned off and that there are no plumbing leaks.
Of the following possible reasons for this inspection, which is probably the MOST important reason?

    A. If the floor gets wet, someone might slip and fall the next morning.
    B. A running water tap might be a sign that there is an intruder in the building.
    C. A washroom flood could leak through the ceilings and walls below and cause a lot of damage.
    D. Leaks must be reported quickly so that repairs can be scheduled as soon as possible.

17.____

18. You are on duty at a public building. A department supervisor tells you that someone has left a suspicious-looking package in the hallway on his floor. You investigate, and you hear ticking in the parcel. You think it could be a bomb.
The FIRST thing you should do is to

    A. rapidly question employees on this floor to get a description of the person who left the package
    B. write down the description of the package and the name of the department supervisor
    C. notify your security headquarters that there may be a bomb in the building and that all personnel should be evacuated
    D. pick up the package carefully and remove it from the building as quickly as you can

18.____

Questions 19-22.

DIRECTIONS: Answer Questions 19 through 22 on the basis of the Fact Situation and the Report of Arrest form below. Questions 19 through 22 ask how the report form should be filled in based on the information given in the Fact Situation.

FACT SITUATION

Jesse Stein is a special officer (security officer) who is assigned to a welfare center at 435 East Smythe Street, Brooklyn. He was on duty there Thursday morning, February 1. At 10:30 A.M., a client named Jo Ann Jones, 40 years old, arrived with her ten-year-old son, Peter. Another client, Mary Alice Wiell, 45 years old, immediately began to insult Mrs. Jones. When Mrs. Jones told her to "go away," Mrs. Wiell pulled out a long knife. The special officer (security officer) intervened and requested Mrs. Wiell to drop the knife. She would not, and he had to use necessary force to disarm her. He arrested her on charges of disorderly conduct, harassment, and possession of a dangerous weapon. Mrs. Wiell lives at 118 Heally Street,

Brooklyn, Apartment 4F, and she is unemployed. The reason for her aggressive behavior is not known.

```
┌─────────────────────────────────────────────────────────────────────────┐
│ REPORT OF ARREST                                                        │
│                                                                         │
│  01) _____    (08) _____  │
│      (Prisoner's surname) (first) (initial)    (Precinct)               │
│                                                                         │
│  (02) _____    (09) _____  │
│       (Address)                               (Date of arrest)          │
│                                               (Month, Day)              │
│                                                                         │
│  (03) _____ (04) _____ (05) _____   (10) _____  │
│      (Date of birth)  (Age)      (Sex)         (Time of arrest)         │
│                                                                         │
│  (06) _____ (07) _____      (11) _____  │
│      (Occupation)   (Where employed)           (Place of arrest)        │
│                                                                         │
│  (12) _____        │
│       (Specific offenses)                                               │
│                                                                         │
│  (13) _____    (14) _____  │
│       (Arresting Officer)                    (Officer's No.)            │
└─────────────────────────────────────────────────────────────────────────┘
```

19. What entry should be made in Blank 01?

    A. Jo Ann Jones B. Jones, Jo Ann
    C. Mary Wiell   D. Wiell, Mary A.

20. Which of the following should be entered in Blank 04?

    A. 40   B. 40's   C. 45   D. Middle-aged

21. Which of the following should be entered in Blank 09?

    A. Wednesday, February 1, 10:30 A.M.
    B. February 1
    C. Thursday morning, February 2
    D. Morning, February 4

22. Of the following, which would be the BEST entry to make in Blank 11?

    A. Really Street Welfare Center
    B. Brooklyn
    C. 435 E. Smythe St., Brooklyn
    D. 118 Healy St., Apt. 4F

Questions 23-27.

DIRECTIONS: Answer Questions 23 through 27 on the basis of the information given in the Report of Loss or Theft that appears below.

```
| REPORT OF LOSS OR THEFT            Date: 12/4    Time: 9:15 a.m. |
| Complaint made by: Richard Aldridge          [ ] Owner           |
|                    306 S. Walter St.         [x] Other - explain:|
|                                              Head of Accty. Dept.|
```

Type of property: _Computer_   Value: _$550.00_
Description: _Dell_
Location: _768 N Margin Ave., Accounting Dept., 3rd Floor_
Time: _Overnight 12/3 - 12/4_
Circumstances: _Mr. Aldridge reports he arrived at work 8:45 A.M., found office door open and machine missing. Nothing else reported missing. I investigated and found signs of forced entry: door lock was broken._   Signature of Reporting Officer: _B.L. Ramirez_

Notify:
[ ] Building & Grounds Office, 768 N. Margin Ave.
[ ] Lost Property Office, 110 Brand Ave.
[x] Security Office, 703 N. Wide Street

23. The person who made this complaint is

    A. a secretary   B. a security officer
    C. Richard Aldridge   D. B.L. Ramirez

24. The report concerns a computer that has been

    A. lost   B. damaged   C. stolen   D. sold

25. The person who took the computer probably entered the office through

    A. a door   B. a window   C. the roof   D. the basement

26. When did the head of the Accounting Department first notice that the computer was missing?

    A. December 4 at 9:15 A.M.   B. December 4 at 8:45 A.M.
    C. The night of December 3   D. The night of December 4

27. The event described in the report took place at

    A. 306 South Walter Street   B. 768 North Margin Avenue
    C. 110 Brand Avenue   D. 703 North Wide Street

Questions 28-33.

DIRECTIONS: Answer Questions 28 through 33 on the basis of the instructions, the code, and the sample question given below.

Assume that a special officer (security officer) at a certain location is equipped with a two-way radio to keep him in constant touch with his security headquarters. Radio messages and replies are given in code form, as follows:

Radio Code for Situation	J	P	M	F	B
Radio Code for Action to be Taken	o	r	a	z	q
Radio Response for Action Being Taken	1	2	3	4	5

Assume that each of the above capital letters is the radio code for a particular type of situation, that the small letter below each capital letter is the radio code for the action a special officer (security officer) is directed to take, and that the number directly below each small letter is the radio response a special officer (security officer) should make to indicate what action was actually taken.

In each of the following Questions 28 through 33, the code letter for the action directed (Column 2) and the code number for the action taken (Column 3) should correspond to the capital letters in Column 1.

If only Column 2 is different from Column 1, mark your answer A.

If only Column 3 is different from Column 1, mark your answer B.

If both Column 2 and Column 3 are different from Column 1, mark your answer C.

If both Columns 2 and 3 are the same as Column 1, mark your answer D.

SAMPLE QUESTION

Column 1	Column 2	Column 3
JPFMB	orzaq	12453

The code letters in Column 2 are correct, but the numbers 53 in Column 3 should be 35. Therefore, the answer is B.

	Column 1	Column 2	Column 3	
28.	PBFJM	rqzoa	25413	28._____
29.	MPFBJ	zrqao	32541	29._____
30.	JBFPM	oqzra	15432	30._____
31.	BJPMF	qaroz	51234	31._____
32.	PJFMB	rozaq	21435	32._____
33.	FJBMP	zoqra	41532	33._____

Questions 34-40.

DIRECTIONS: Questions 34 through 40 are based on the instructions given below. Study the instructions and the sample question; then answer Questions 34 through 40 on the basis of this information

INSTRUCTIONS:

In each of the following Questions 34 through 40, the 3-line name and address in Column 1 is the master-list entry, and the 3-line entry in Column 2 is the information to be checked against the master list.

If there is one line that does not match, mark your answer A.

If there are two lines that do not match, mark your answer B.

If all three lines do not match, mark your answer C.

If the lines all match exactly, mark your answer D.

SAMPLE QUESTION:

Column 1
Mark L. Field
11-09 Prince Park Blvd.
Bronx, N.Y. 11402

Column 2
Mark L. Field
11-99 Prince Park
Bronx, N.Y. 11401

The first lines in each column match exactly. The second lines do not match, since 11-09 does not match 11-99 and Blvd. does not match Way. The third lines do not match either, since 11402 does not match 11401. Therefore, there are two lines that do not match and the correct answer is B.

	Column 1	Column 2	
34.	Jerome A. Jackson 1243 14th Avenue New York, N.Y. 10023	Jerome A. Johnson 1234 14th Avenue New York, N.Y. 10023	34.____
35.	Sophie Strachtheim 33-28 Connecticut Ave. Far Rockaway, N.Y. 11697	Sophie Strachtheim 33-28 Connecticut Ave. Far Rockaway, N.Y. 11697	35.____
36.	Elisabeth N.T. Gorrell 256 Exchange St. New York, N.Y. 10013	Elizabeth N.T. Gorrell 256 Exchange St. New York, N.Y. 10013	36.____
37.	Maria J. Gonzalez 7516 E. Sheepshead Rd. Brooklyn, N.Y. 11240	Maria J. Gonzalez 7516 N. Shepshead Rd. Brooklyn, N.Y. 11240	37.____
38.	Leslie B. Brautenweiler 21 57A Seller Terr. Flushing, N.Y. 11367	Leslie B. Brautenwieler 21-75A Seiler Terr. Flushing, N.J. 11367	38.____

39. Rigoberto J. Peredes 157 Twin Towers, #18F Tottenville, S.I., N.Y.	Rigoberto J. Peredes 157 Twin Towers, #18F Tottenville, S.I., N.Y.	39._____
40. Pietro F. Albino P.O. Box 7548 Floral Park, N.Y. 11005	Pietro F. Albina P.O. Box 7458 Floral Park, N.Y. 11005	40._____

KEY (CORRECT ANSWERS)

1.	D	11.	A	21.	B	31.	A
2.	C	12.	D	22.	C	32.	D
3.	B	13.	C	23.	C	33.	A
4.	D	14.	B	24.	C	34.	B
5.	B	15.	A	25.	A	35.	D
6.	A	16.	C	26.	B	36.	A
7.	C	17.	C	27.	B	37.	A
8.	D	18.	C	28.	D	38.	C
9.	D	19.	D	29.	C	39.	D
10.	D	20.	C	30.	B	40.	B

EXAMINATION SECTION
TEST 1

DIRECTIONS: Each question or incomplete statement is followed by several suggested answers or completions. Select the one that BEST answers the question or completes the statement. *PRINT THE LETTER OF THE CORRECT ANSWER IN THE SPACE AT THE RIGHT.*

1. Which of the following is the LEAST important factor to consider in surveying the physical layout of a building for traffic flow? 1.____

    A. Location of windows
    B. Number of entrances
    C. Number of exits
    D. Location of first aid rooms

2. The major purpose of any security program in a large organization is to prevent unlawful acts. 2.____
   If adequate patrol coverage is provided at a given location, it is MOST likely that

    A. crimes will not be committed
    B. undesirables will not enter the building
    C. unlawful acts will increase in the long run
    D. there will be less opportunity to commit a crime

3. The MOST frequent cause of fires in public facilities is 3.____

    A. incinerators   B. vandalism
    C. electrical sources   D. smoking on the job

4. After bomb threats are received, it is sometimes necessary to evacuate a facility. How long BEFORE the threatened time of explosion should a facility be evacuated? 4.____
   At least _____ minutes.

    A. 15   B. 25   C. 50   D. 60

5. Once a facility is evacuated because of a bomb threat, how much time should pass before the public and employees are allowed to enter the building? 5.____
   _____ minutes.

    A. 10   B. 20   C. 40   D. 60

6. Of the following locations in public buildings, the one which is the LEAST likely place for bombs to be planted is in 6.____

    A. storerooms   B. bathrooms
    C. cafeterias   D. waste receptacles

7. The one of the following that is the surest means of establishing positive identification of someone entering a facility is by 7.____

    A. personal recognition   B. I.D. badge
    C. social security card   D. driver's license

55

8. The one of the following which most probably would NOT be included in a police record report concerning an incident at a facility is the

   A. name of complainant or injured party
   B. name of the investigating officer
   C. statement of each witness
   D. religion of complainant or injured party

9. Preventing trouble is one of the primary concerns of special officers.
   When dealing with unruly groups of people who threaten to become violent, which of the following is a measure which should NOT be taken?

   A. Maintain close surveillance of such groups
   B. Try to contact the leaders of the group regardless of their militancy
   C. Keep the officer force alerted
   D. Have the officer force deal aggressively with provocations

10. Of the following, the MOST important factor to consider in the deployment of officers dealing with a client population is the officers' ability to

    A. remain calm
    B. look stern
    C. evaluate personality
    D. take a firm stand

11. Assume that an offender is struggling with a group of officers who are trying to arrest him.
    What force, if any, can be used to overcome this resistance?

    A. The amount of force acceptable to the public
    B. The amount of force necessary to restrain the offender and protect the officers
    C. Any amount of force that is acceptable to the officers at the scene
    D. No force may be used until the police arrive

12. Assume that a fire is discovered at your work location. The one of the following actions which would be INAPPROPRIATE for you to take is to

    A. notify the telephone operator
    B. station a reliable person at the entrance
    C. open all windows and doors in the area
    D. start evacuating the area

13. If a person has an object caught in his throat or air passage but is breathing adequately, which one of the following should you do?

    A. Probe for the object
    B. Force him to drink water
    C. Lay him over your arm and slap him between the shoulder blades
    D. Allow him to cough and to assume the position he finds most comfortable

14. The one of the following methods which should NOT be used to report a fire is to

    A. call 911
    B. pull the handle in the red box on the street corner
    C. call the fire department county numbers listed in each county directory
    D. call 411

15. Assume that an officer, alone in a building at night, smells the strong odor of cooking or heating gas. In addition to airing the building and making sure that he is not overcome, it would be BEST for the officer to call

    A. his superior at his home and ask for instructions
    B. for a plumber from the department of public works
    C. 911 for police and fire help
    D. the emergency number at Con Edison

16. Of the following situations, the one that is MOST dangerous for an officer is when he

    A. investigates suspicious persons and circumstances
    B. finds a burglary in progress or pursues burglary suspects
    C. attempts an arrest or finds a robbery in progress
    D. patrols on the overnight shift

17. An officer on security patrol generally should spend MOST of his time

    A. checking doors and locks
    B. helping the public and answering questions
    C. chasing criminals and looking for clues
    D. writing reports on unusual incidents

18. The one of the following that is an ACCEPTABLE way to arrest a person is to

    A. tell him to report to the nearest police precinct
    B. send a summons to his permanent address
    C. tell him in person that he is under arrest
    D. show him handcuffs and ask him to come along

19. A carbon dioxide fire extinguisher is BEST suited for extinguishing _____ fires.

    A. paper   B. rag   C. rubbish   D. grease

20. A pressurized water or soda-acid fire extinguisher is BEST suited for extinguishing _____ fires.

    A. wood   B. gasoline
    C. electrical   D. magnesium

21. The one of the following statements that does NOT apply to the use of handcuffs is that they

    A. are used as temporary restraining devices
    B. eliminate the need for vigilance
    C. cannot be opened without keys
    D. are used to secure a violent person

22. The one of the following that is GENERALLY a crime against the person is

    A. trespass   B. burglary   C. robbery   D. arson

23. Of the following, the SAFEST way of escape from an office in a burning building is generally the

    A. stairway
    B. rooftop
    C. passenger elevator
    D. freight elevator

24. In attempting to control a possible riot situation, an officer pushed his way into a crowd gathered outside the building and tried to cause confusion by arguing with members of the group.
    This procedure NORMALLY is considered

    A. *desirable;* any violence that occurs will remain outside the building
    B. *desirable;* the crowd will break into smaller groups and disperse
    C. *undesirable;* to maintain control of the situation, the officer must not become part of the crowd
    D. *undesirable;* the supervisor should stay clear of the scene

25. Which one of the following is MOST effective in making officers more safety-minded?

    A. Maintaining an up-to-date library of the latest safety literature
    B. Reading daily safety bulletins at roll-call
    C. Holding informal group safety meetings periodically
    D. Offering prizes for good safety slogans and displays

KEY (CORRECT ANSWERS)

1.	A	11.	B
2.	D	12.	C
3.	C	13.	D
4.	A	14.	D
5.	D	15.	D
6.	C	16.	C
7.	A	17.	A
8.	D	18.	C
9.	D	19.	D
10.	A	20.	A

21.	B
22.	C
23.	A
24.	C
25.	C

TEST 2

DIRECTIONS: Each question or incomplete statement is followed by several suggested answers or completions. Select the one that BEST answers the question or completes the statement. *PRINT THE LETTER OF THE CORRECT ANSWER IN THE SPACE AT THE RIGHT.*

1. Assume that an angry crowd of some 75 to 100 people has built up in one of the hallways of a center and that only one superior officer and two subordinate officers are on duty in the building. A glass panel in one of the stairway doors has just been broken under the pressure of the crowd and a bench has been hurled down a flight of stairs. The one of the following actions that the superior officer SHOULD take in this situation is to

   A. push his way into the crowd and try to reason with them
   B. order the two other officers to try to quiet the crowd
   C. call the police on 911 and meet them outside the building
   D. do nothing at this point in order to avoid a riot

2. One of the duties and responsibilities of a supervisor is to test the knowledge of the officers concerning their post conditions.
   This should be done if the officer's assignment is

   A. fixed only
   B. roving only
   C. roving only in a troublesome spot
   D. either fixed or roving

3. An officer discovers early one morning that an office in the building he guards has been burglarized.
   Of the following, it is important for the officer to FIRST

   A. go through the building and look for suspects
   B. call the police and protect the area and whatever evidence exists until they arrive
   C. allow people into their offices as they come to work
   D. examine, sort, and handle all evidence before the police get there

4. Assume that two officers are interrogating one suspect. How should these officers position themselves during the interrogation?

   A. One officer should stand on either side of the suspect.
   B. One officer should stand to the right of the suspect, and the other officer should stand behind the suspect.
   C. Both officers should stand to the right of the suspect.
   D. One officer should stand to the right of the suspect, and the other officer should stand in front of the suspect.

5. A witness who takes an oath to testify truly and who states as true any matter which he knows to be false is guilty of

   A. perjury   B. libel   C. slander   D. fraud

6. An officer checking a substance suspected of containing narcotics should GENERALLY

   A. taste it in small amounts
   B. send it to a laboratory for analysis
   C. smell it for its distinctive odor
   D. examine it for its unusual texture

7. A certain center is situated in an area where frequent outbreaks of hostilities seem to be focused on the center itself.
Which of the following BEST explains why the center may be a target for hostile acts?
It

   A. serves community needs
   B. represents governmental authority
   C. represents all ethnic groups
   D. serves as a neutral battlefield

8. An officer often deals with people who might be addicted to drugs.
The one of the following symptoms which is NOT generally an indication of drug addiction is

   A. dilation of the eye pupils
   B. frequent yawning and sneezing
   C. a deep, rasping cough
   D. continual itching of the arms and legs

9. In emergency situations, panic will MOST probably occur when people are

   A. unexpectedly confronted with a terrorizing condition from which there appears to be no escape
   B. angry and violent
   C. anxious about circumstances which are not obvious, easily visible or within the immediate area
   D. familiar with the effects of the emergency

10. The one of the following actions on the part of a person that would NOT be considered *resisting arrest* is

    A. retreating and running away
    B. saying, *You can't arrest me*
    C. pushing the officer aside
    D. pulling away from an officer's grasp

11. Which of the following items would NOT be considered an APPROPRIATE item of uniform for an officer to wear while on duty?

    A. Reefer type overcoat
    B. Leather laced shoes with flat soles
    C. White socks
    D. Cap cover with cap device displayed

12. What can happen to an officer if the leather thong on his night stick is NOT twisted correctly?
    The

    A. baton may be taken out of the officer's hand
    B. officer's wrist may be broken
    C. leather will tear more easily
    D. officer's arm may be injured

13. The one of the following kinds of information which SHOULD be included in the log book is

    A. any important matter of police information
    B. an item noted in Standard Operating Procedures only
    C. everything of general interest
    D. a crime or offense only

14. While on patrol at your work location, you receive a call that an assault has taken place. Upon your arrival at the scene, the victim, who has severe lacerations, informs you that the assailant ran into a nearby basement.
    After apprehending the suspect, the type of search you should conduct is a _____ search.

    A. wall   B. frisk   C. body   D. strip

15. A tactical force is valuable in MOST emergency situations PRIMARILY because of its

    A. location   B. morale
    C. flexibility   D. size

16. An officer should be encouraged to talk easily and frankly when he is dealing with his superior.
    In order to encourage such free communication, it would be MOST appropriate for a superior to behave in a(n)

    A. *sincere* manner; assure the officer that you will deal with him honestly and openly
    B. *official* manner; you are a superior officer and must always act formally with subordinates
    C. *investigative* manner; you must probe and question to get to a basis of trust
    D. *unemotional* manner; the officer's emotions and background should play no part in your dealings with him

17. Research findings show that an increase in free communication within an agency GENERALLY results in which one of the following?

    A. Improved morale and productivity
    B. Increased promotional opportunities
    C. An increase in authority
    D. A spirit of honesty

18. Assume that you are a superior officer and your superiors have given you a new arrest procedure to be followed. Before passing this information on to your subordinates, the one of the following actions that you should take FIRST is to

    A. ask your superiors to send out a memorandum to the entire staff
    B. clarify the procedure in your own mind
    C. set up a training course to provide instructions on the new procedure
    D. write a memorandum to your subordinates

19. Communication is necessary for an organization to be effective.
    The one of the following which is LEAST important for most communication systems is that

    A. messages are sent quickly and directly to the person who needs them to operate
    B. information should be conveyed understandably and accurately
    C. the method used to transmit information should be kept secret so that security can be maintained
    D. senders of messages must know how their messages were received and acted upon

20. Which one of the following is the CHIEF advantage of listening willingly to subordinate officers and encouraging them to talk freely and honestly?
    It

    A. reveals to superiors the degree to which ideas that are passed down are accepted by subordinates
    B. reduces the participation of subordinates in the operation of the department
    C. encourages officers to try for promotion
    D. enables officers to learn about security leaks on the part of officials

21. A superior may be informed through either oral or written reports.
    Which one of the following is an ADVANTAGE of using oral reports?

    A. There is no need for a formal record of the report.
    B. An exact duplicate of the report is not easily transmitted to others.
    C. A good oral report requires little time for preparation.
    D. An oral report involves two-way communication between a subordinate and his superior.

22. Of the following, the MOST important reason why officers should communicate effectively with the public is to

    A. improve the public's understanding of information that is important for them to know
    B. establish a friendly relationship
    C. obtain information about the kinds of people who come to the center
    D. convince the public that services are adequate

23. Officers should generally NOT use phrases like *too hard, too easy,* and *a lot* principally because such phrases

    A. may be offensive to some minority groups
    B. are too informal

C. mean different things to different people
D. are difficult to remember

24. The ability to communicate clearly and concisely is an important element in effective leadership.
Which of the following statements about oral and written communication is GENERALLY true?

A. Oral communication is more time-consuming.
B. Written communication is more likely to be misinterpreted.
C. Oral communication is useful only in emergencies.
D. Written communication is useful mainly when giving information to fewer than twenty people.

25. Rumors can often have harmful and disruptive effects on an organization.
Which one of the following is the BEST way to prevent rumors from becoming a problem?

A. Refuse to act on rumors, thereby making them less believable
B. Increase the amount of information passed along by the *grapevine*
C. Distribute as much factual information as possible
D. Provide training in report writing

KEY (CORRECT ANSWERS)

1.	C	11.	C
2.	D	12.	A
3.	B	13.	A
4.	B	14.	A
5.	A	15.	C
6.	B	16.	A
7.	B	17.	A
8.	C	18.	B
9.	A	19.	C
10.	B	20.	A

21. D
22. A
23. C
24. B
25. C

EXAMINATION SECTION
TEST 1

DIRECTIONS: Each question or incomplete statement is followed by several suggested answers or completions. Select the one that BEST answers the question or completes the statement. *PRINT THE LETTER OF THE CORRECT ANSWER IN THE SPACE AT THE RIGHT.*

1. When training your subordinates in a new method of crowd control, which one of the following techniques SHOULD be used?

    A. Teach them the whole job at one time, whether it contains a great many steps or only a few
    B. Issue orders without giving reasons because this will result in more questions and delays
    C. Explain and demonstrate, one step at a time
    D. Use technical language in order to make instructions precise

2. It is sometimes necessary to provide additional training for staff members who are poor in their performance of specific tasks.
Of the following, the MOST effective way of improving staff performance is to

    A. use visual aids along with reading material to train staff on the general subject involved
    B. train subordinates to perform only those tasks which they normally perform
    C. plan and carry out programs to meet the subordinates' real work needs
    D. provide training only for staff members performing critical tasks

3. Assume that as a superior officer you confront one of your subordinate officers with the fact that he is not performing his job effectively. The officer tries to avoid the blame and shifts the criticism to other officers including yourself.
Which one of the following is NOT a good way of handling this situation?

    A. Speaking and acting in an impartial and fair-minded manner
    B. Trying to determine why the officer finds it difficult to accept justifiable criticism
    C. Calling in the other officers whom this subordinate has criticized and having them discuss the matter with him
    D. Listening to the officer, at least at the outset, rather than interrupting his statement

4. For a superior officer to discuss a subordinate's performance evaluation with him is GENERALLY

    A. *inadvisable;* such a discussion will discourage a good worker
    B. *advisable;* the subordinate must know about the quality of his performance for improvement to occur
    C. *inadvisable;* a good performance evaluation will result in the subordinate's asking for more responsibility
    D. *advisable;* such discussions generally lead to a change in the subordinate's evaluation

5. The one of the following which is the MAJOR cause of employee lateness is

   A. low morale
   B. excessive fatigue
   C. accidents
   D. sickness

6. For officers to work together smoothly, teamwork is necessary.
   Which one of the following statements BEST describes the relationship between leadership and teamwork?

   A. Leadership cannot exist without teamwork.
   B. Teamwork cannot exist without leadership.
   C. Leadership and teamwork are one and the same.
   D. There is no relationship between leadership and teamwork.

7. For superiors who wish to achieve proper discipline among subordinates, it is generally MOST difficult to

   A. obtain rapid compliance with orders and directives
   B. prevent subordinates from questioning orders that are issued to them
   C. achieve compliance with orders while encouraging individual initiative
   D. use punishment to prevent infractions of the rules

8. Of the following, it is MOST likely that laxity in administering discipline will result in

   A. a loss of respect for their superior on the part of subordinates
   B. the satisfactory completion of the organization's job
   C. an increase in the number of disturbances at centers
   D. the establishment of proper conditions for successful administration

9. In dealing with a subordinate who shows a lack of interest in performing his duties, a superior officer should GENERALLY

   A. assign to him all the difficult work
   B. give him more responsibility
   C. inspect his performance more often than usual
   D. give him direct, detailed orders

10. A superior officer who has a highly motivated group of officers under his command GENERALLY

    A. shows an interest in how they are doing and is willing to back them up
    B. spends most of his time in closely supervising his subordinates
    C. supervises mainly through one of his subordinate officers
    D. is management-oriented rather than subordinate-oriented

11. As a superior, you might have to supervise subordinate officers who are very enthusiastic and ambitious.
    Which one of the following is the BEST reason for carefully watching the work of such officers?
    They

    A. may produce so much work that other officers resent them
    B. may appear to be overly concerned about being promoted
    C. might make decisions before obtaining the necessary information
    D. may be seeking the superior's job

12. In dealing with the public, officers should behave with courtesy.
    Which one of the following practices would be LEAST effective in promoting courtesy?

    A. Giving advice on subjects about which you are not well informed
    B. Learning to take constructive criticism intelligently
    C. Avoiding discussions of a personal nature
    D. Treating members of the public as you would like to be treated

13. When directing the officers under your command, which one of the following is generally the MOST effective method of supervision?

    A. Provide your directions through written orders to prevent misunderstanding
    B. Supervise every detail of the work closely so that it is carried out exactly as you want it
    C. Limit your concern to getting the job done and not to the people doing the work
    D. Set up general standards and goals so that officers have leeway as to how to achieve them

14. Leadership is particularly important in the security field.
    Of the following, people GENERALLY expect their leader to

    A. state, *Do as I say, not as I do*
    B. refuse to allow changes in orders
    C. get many of his ideas from his subordinates
    D. take his feelings out on those who make mistakes

15. The MOST important single factor in the selection of a person for assignment to a position of greater responsibility should be his

    A. demonstrated ability to do the job
    B. schooling, both civilian and military
    C. training and experience on the job
    D. length of service

16. Security training received by security officers and noted in their personnel charts or records should NOT be used as a basis for

    A. indicating individual degrees of skill
    B. assigning officers to particular shifts
    C. establishing priorities of instruction
    D. presenting a consolidated picture of the training status

17. As a superior officer, you note that one of your subordinates has not been performing his job properly. You discover that the cause of this problem seems to be that he drinks excessively when off duty.
    Of the following, the BEST way to handle this situation is to

    A. discipline the officer to the fullest extent possible
    B. discuss the problem and possible solutions with the officer's fellow workers
    C. wait until the officer has straightened himself out and then counsel him
    D. have a blunt and firm talk with the officer and direct him to seek treatment

18. Officers who are overly sensitive to criticism are one of the problems that superiors must deal with.
Of the following, which is the BEST way to handle such officers?
They should

   A. not be talked to differently from other officers
   B. be criticized only on serious mistakes
   C. not be criticized at all
   D. be reassured of their worth to their unit

19. A superior officer who suspects an employee of petty office theft calls the employee to his office and questions him directly.
In this situation, the superior's action is

   A. *desirable,* primarily because the subordinate should be allowed to answer these accusations privately
   B. *desirable,* primarily because confrontation will persuade the employee to tell the truth
   C. *undesirable,* primarily because line department personnel should handle such matters
   D. *undesirable,* primarily because direct confrontation might unnecessarily embarrass the employee

20. Assume that a certain superior officer assigns a task, without explanation, to a new subordinate who is not yet accepted by the work group.
Of the following, the MOST likely result of this action would be to

   A. encourage the subordinate to perform at his best
   B. make the subordinate feel insecure about proving himself
   C. stimulate other officers to do their best to impress the new staff member
   D. cause the experienced officers to feel inferior

21. A newly appointed superior officer often faces the problem of supervising officers who were formerly close personal friends of his.
In this situation, the one of the following which is the BEST approach to take toward these officers is to

   A. break all ties with former friends
   B. stay personally close with friends as this is always an advantage on the job
   C. maintain a relationship of easy, occasional familiarity
   D. become businesslike on the job but remain close socially

22. Assume that you, as a superior officer, are talking over a proposed change in procedure with your subordinates which would require their full cooperation.
Which one of the following actions would be MOST appropriate for you to take if your subordinates suggest modifications in the procedure?

   A. Prepare arguments against your subordinates' suggestions while you are listening to them
   B. Refuse to accept suggestions for changes since procedures can't be modified
   C. Listen carefully since your subordinates' suggestions may have merit
   D. Accept the recommendations of your more experienced subordinates

23. The successful supervisor should be aware that two of his most important assets are patience and understanding.
Of the following actions by a supervisor, the one that is LEAST likely to demonstrate these qualities would be to

    A. make deadlines realistic and reachable
    B. reprimand an employee the minute he makes a mistake
    C. assist employees in work-related problems
    D. discuss changes in procedures with subordinates

24. One of a supervisor's goals should be to create and maintain a force of loyal subordinates with high morale. This objective is likely to be achieved by all of the following EXCEPT

    A. making subordinate officers feel that their job is an important one
    B. encouraging supervisors to be concerned with the individual needs of subordinates
    C. giving subordinate officers an opportunity to express their thoughts, likes, and interests to their supervisors
    D. having supervisors rely only on the advice of trusted employees when resolving disputes between subordinates

25. One of a supervisor's major responsibilities is to evaluate the performance of his subordinates.
Which one of the following practices would be LEAST productive in developing meaningful evaluations from performance interviews?

    A. Make positive statements only
    B. Outline the points to discuss
    C. Adjust to the individual and situation
    D. Allow the employee to participate

KEY (CORRECT ANSWERS)

1. C
2. C
3. C
4. B
5. A

6. B
7. C
8. A
9. B
10. A

11. C
12. A
13. D
14. C
15. A

16. B
17. D
18. D
19. A
20. B

21. C
22. C
23. B
24. D
25. A

TEST 2

DIRECTIONS: Each question or incomplete statement is followed by several suggested answers or completions. Select the one that BEST answers the question or completes the statement. *PRINT THE LETTER OF THE COREECT ANSWER IN THE SPACE AT THE RIGHT.*

1. Assume that you are a superior officer concerned with improving the attitude of your subordinates toward their work.
   Of the following, the action that is MOST likely to improve this attitude would be for you to

   A. allow your subordinates to take extra time off
   B. interpret rules and regulations leniently
   C. request a merit increase in salary for your subordinates
   D. train your subordinates to perform at the highest possible level

   1.____

2. Assume that two of the officers under your command are hotly disputing the accuracy of a log book entry. One of the officers asks for your opinion.
   Which of the following would be LEAST advisable for you to do in this situation?

   A. Ask the officers to present their views calmly
   B. Keep your temper and remain impartial
   C. Stop the argument and then give your decision
   D. Judge the argument in proportion to its importance

   2.____

3. A superior officer notices that one of his subordinates is not doing his job.
   In this situation, it would be MOST appropriate for the superior officer to

   A. caution the subordinate officer promptly
   B. ignore the incident this time
   C. check on the subordinate officer's behavior in an hour
   D. warn the subordinate officer at the end of his work day that a report may be filed

   3.____

4. A recently appointed superior officer finds it difficult to make the decisions required in his new position.
   Which one of the following suggestions would be MOST helpful to him in overcoming this problem?

   A. Don't be concerned because everyone makes mistakes, and any mistake caused by your decisions will be ignored.
   B. Remember that you will be judged by the long-range soundness of all of your decisions.
   C. Since you are now in charge of a number of officers, let them bear the decision-making responsibility.
   D. Remember that you have a superior and that he can make the decision for you.

   4.____

5. Of the following, the BEST reason for a superior officer to nake inspections and rounds is to

   A. observe the physical appearance of personnel
   B. determine whether communication equipment is working properly

   5.____

C. decide whether adequate records are being kept
D. see that the performance of subordinates conforms with departmental standards

6. Assume that you, as a superior officer, have made an inspection and have submitted recommendations for improvements.
Which one of the following actions should be taken to assure that the desired results are obtained from the inspection?
You should

   A. distribute copies of the recommendations to all members of the force
   B. follow-up to determine whether the recommended improvements have been made
   C. give credit to other officers when it is due in order to help increase morale
   D. set up a schedule so that you inspect once a week

7. Assume that you have noticed that one of your subordinates has been quiet and rather depressed for two to three days with no change in his usual satisfactory job performance.
Of the following, the BEST action for you to take in this situation is to

   A. ask him to describe his feelings in detail
   B. act as if you noticed no change in the subordinate's behavior
   C. tell him to forget what's bothering him
   D. recommend that he seek professional guidance

8. Assume that you wish to introduce a change in your subordinates' work procedures in order to improve their performance.
Of the following, the BEST way to gain acceptance of this change is for you to

   A. stress its positive aspects
   B. downgrade past practices
   C. delay discussing it for a while
   D. order your subordinates to follow the new procedure at once

9. Suppose you come across two of your subordinate officers having an argument about the boundaries of their patrol posts.
Which of the following is the LEAST advisable course of action for you to take after stopping the argument?

   A. Tell the officers to speak with you individually
   B. Have the officers submit their views in writing for you to evaluate properly when you have time
   C. Meet with both officers in your office after they finish their tours
   D. Tell the officers to consult you on such matters in the future

10. Assume that a superior officer is explaining a new rule to his men at roll call. One officer states that he does not like the rule. The superior tells the officer that he agrees with him, but that the rule must be followed anyway. In this situation, the superior officer's statement was

    A. *proper*, chiefly because the men should know where superiors stand on rules and regulations
    B. *improper,* chiefly because superiors should not indicate disagreement with a change in rules since they must enforce them

C. *proper,* chiefly because efficiency improves when supervisors and subordinates agree on new rules
D. *improper,* chiefly because questions regarding rule changes should be answered at staff meetings rather than at roll call

11. Assume that you find that several of your subordinate officers have not performed satisfactorily during the last few emergency situations at your work location. The one of the following actions which is LEAST likely to improve their performance is for you to

    A. keep the subordinates informed about how they performed after each emergency
    B. stay alert for officers who are having difficulty with their work
    C. circulate among the officers at emergencies
    D. avoid the use of criticism

11._____

12. Of the following qualifications for an officer, the one that is MOST important is the ability to

    A. understand and get along with people
    B. write a good report
    C. overcome resistance to arrest
    D. solve crimes

12._____

13. Assume that you have noticed that one of your subordinate officers makes errors when questioning clients. You discuss with him the proper method to use when questioning clients.
Of the following, your NEXT step should be to

    A. ask another officer to check on your subordinate's procedure when questioning clients
    B. tell the officer to discuss with others how they question clients
    C. have the officer report regularly to you about the clients he questions
    D. watch the officer to see how he questions clients

13._____

14. One of the MOST important rules to follow when communicating with your superior is:

    A. Report everything that happens at your work location to him
    B. Pass on to him rumors and gossip heard within your center
    C. Let him hear from you first about any unusual success, problem or error
    D. Assign to one of your subordinates the responsibility of communicating with your supervisor

14._____

15. A superior officer may be required to instruct subordinates in the performance of their tasks.
Which of the following would NOT be proper when instructing a small group of employees?

    A. Use simple language
    B. Explain the procedure and the reason for the procedure
    C. Demonstrate one step at a time
    D. Use the lecture method instead of the discussion method whenever possible

15._____

4 (#2)

16. Assume that a new officer has joined your unit. Which of the following approaches should you, as his superior officer, use in introducing him to the job?

   A. Put him right to work; he will learn best through his mistakes
   B. Act sternly, thereby gaining his respect and indicating the proper supervisor-subordinate relationship
   C. Give him the overall picture of the department and unit he is in
   D. Praise him, even when he makes errors, in order to gain his confidence

17. When a new officer begins work, he will often perform tasks ineffectively, thus requiring corrective action by his supervisor.
    In this situation, which one of the following represents the MOST desirable course of action for the supervisor?

   A. Point out specific errors in performance and how to correct them
   B. Tell the new officer that he is not doing the job properly and assign him to a new task
   C. Avoid criticism in the beginning since it may result in bitterness
   D. Do not criticize because criticism is not currently considered an acceptable tool of management

18. Of the following types of work, the one that is MOST likely to lead to dissatisfaction is work that is

   A. difficult to perform   B. tiring to complete
   C. uncomplicated   D. unimportant

19. When instructing subordinates to perform new tasks, the one of the following that is LEAST important in helping then to learn is to

   A. explain the procedure to them in a step-by-step manner
   B. show them what they must do
   C. let them do the task under guidance
   D. have them perform the task without supervision so they may learn from their mistakes

20. Which one of the following is the MOST important single thing to bear in mind about giving orders?

   A. An order should be given to a capable employee, not an uncooperative one.
   B. If an order is given correctly, you will not have to check the work.
   C. An order should be given in as forceful a manner as possible to assure that it is understood.
   D. An order is given because it is necessary to bring about certain results.

21. Suppose that a subordinate asks you about a rumor he has heard. The rumor deals with a subject which your superiors consider *confidential*.
    Which of the following BEST describes how you should answer the officer?
    Tell

   A. the officer that you don't make the rules and that he should speak to higher ranking officers
   B. the officer that you will ask your superior for information

C. him only that you cannot comment on the matter
D. him the rumor is not true

22. Superior officers often find it difficult to *get their message across* when instructing newly appointed officers in their various duties.
The MAIN reason for this is generally that the

    A. duties of the officers have increased
    B. superior officer is often so expert in his area that he fails to see it from the learner's point of view
    C. superior officer adapts his instruction to the slowest learner in the group
    D. new officers are younger, less concerned with job security, and more interested in fringe benefits

22.____

23. Assume that you are discussing a security problem with an officer under your command. During the discussion, you see that the officer's eyes are turning away from you and that he is not paying attention.
In order to get the officer's attention, you should FIRST

    A. ask him to look you in the eye
    B. talk to him about sports
    C. tell him he is being very rude
    D. change your tone of voice

23.____

24. As a superior officer, you may find it necessary to conduct meetings with your subordinates.
Of the following, which would be MOST helpful in assuring that a meeting accomplishes the purpose for which it was called?

    A. Give notice of the conclusions you would like to reach at the start of the meeting
    B. Delay the start of the meeting until everyone is present
    C. Write down points to be discussed in proper sequence
    D. Make sure everyone is clear on whatever conclusions have been reached and on what must be done after the meeting

24.____

25. Every superior officer will occasionally be called upon to deliver a reprimand to a subordinate. If done properly, this can greatly help an officer improve his performance.
Which one of the following is NOT a good practice to follow when giving a reprimand?

    A. Maintain your composure and temper
    B. Reprimand a subordinate in the presence of other officers so they can learn the same lesson
    C. Try to understand why the officer was not able to perform satisfactorily
    D. Let your knowledge of the officer involved determine the exact nature of the reprimand

25.____

KEY (CORRECT ANSWERS)

1.	D	11.	D
2.	C	12.	A
3.	A	13.	D
4.	B	14.	C
5.	D	15.	D
6.	B	16.	C
7.	B	17.	A
8.	A	18.	D
9.	B	19.	D
10.	B	20.	D

21. B
22. B
23. D
24. D
25. B

TEST 3

DIRECTIONS: Each question or incomplete statement is followed by several suggested answers or completions. Select the one that BEST answers the question or completes the statement. *PRINT THE LETTER OF THE CORRECT ANSWER IN THE SPACE AT THE RIGHT.*

1. Of the following, the PRIMARY purpose of communications between subordinates and superiors is to

   A. develop language skills
   B. enable subordinates to air their grievances
   C. help establish friendly ties
   D. solve job problems

   1.____

2. Of the following, the MOST necessary elements of good communication are

   A. openness and form
   B. details and subjectivity
   C. speed and dependability
   D. length and appearance

   2.____

3. Of the following, the MOST important role of a supervisor is that of

   A. being able to understand how his men feel about their assignments
   B. establishing good contacts with the administration
   C. fulfilling his responsibility to the assigned position
   D. presenting a good public image on the behalf of his organization

   3.____

4. Of the following, the LEAST desirable behavior of a senior officer would be for him to

   A. attempt to gain the respect of superiors
   B. attempt to find causes of high employee turnover
   C. ignore infrequent latenesses
   D. ignore suggestions which may prove unworthy

   4.____

5. A senior officer who consults with his subordinates about operational planning is GENERALLY

   A. attempting to prove his supervisory ability
   B. developing their job participation and cooperation
   C. passing down his responsibilities to others
   D. searching for an employee with supervisory ability

   5.____

6. If a senior officer conducted supervision and inspection programs in order to become aware of his men's conduct, he would GENERALLY be considered to be

   A. excessively strict and authoritarian
   B. looking for potential troublemakers
   C. overconscientious in his work
   D. performing a vital duty

   6.____

7. Of the following, the BEST reason for a supervisor's evaluation of his own on-the-job performance is to enable him to

   A. find the best methods of supervising his men and in getting the job done
   B. give the impression that he is sincere in trying to become a better supervisor

   7.____

C. make a favorable impression on his superiors
D. make his work seem more important than it actually is

8. Assume that you are a senior officer making a performance evaluation of an officer. The reason for NOT drawing conclusions too quickly is CHIEFLY that

   A. without due consideration of all the facts, you are likely to evaluate the officer on biased personal judgment
   B. evaluation reports take a great deal of time and thought
   C. senior officers must consult with superiors before drawing conclusions about a subordinate's performance
   D. the officer might try to disprove any wrong information which you may have obtained about him

8.____

9. A senior officer notices two officers, known to be good workers, playing practical jokes and pranks on the other employees.
In this case, disciplinary action is

   A. *desirable,* chiefly because horseplay on the job is not, strictly speaking, against the rules
   B. *undesirable,* chiefly because good workers tend to correct their own improper actions
   C. *desirable,* chiefly because horseplay could provoke other employees and that would disrupt normal work routine
   D. *undesirable,* chiefly because a supervisor should not get involved with employees' affairs

9.____

10. Resistance to or resentment of training is likely to be an attitude shown by many officers. Therefore, it is important for a senior officer to understand the causes of his men's attitudes and learn how to deal with them. Of the following, which is the BEST method of lessening an officer's resentment of training?

    A. Give the officers extra time off for taking part in the training program
    B. Openly criticize the officer who often makes mistakes during training
    C. Recommend promotions for those who complete the training program quickest
    D. Explain that the purpose of the training is to help them perform their jobs more efficiently

10.____

11. A senior officer required all officers under his supervision to submit a weekly report based on information from their daily log (memo) entries. The senior officer did not examine these reports, but he did file them as proof that the officers were not *sleeping* on the job.
In general, this practice of the senior officer is considered

    A. *correct,* chiefly because the senior officer has little need of the reports since he is usually on the scene to observe the performance of his men
    B. *incorrect*, chiefly because, if the senior officer asked for reports, he should read or use the information they contain
    C. *correct,* chiefly because any information an officer had could only be based on daily occurrences
    D. *incorrect,* chiefly because the senior officer is placing too much emphasis on accuracy of paper work

11.____

12. Selecting an employee to be trained for performing the supervisor's duties is generally considered

    A. *desirable*, chiefly because it allows the supervisor to avoid many of his duties
    B. *undesirable*, chiefly because it creates the impression that the supervisor is showing favoritism
    C. *desirable*, chiefly because supervisory coverage is assured in the absence of the supervisor
    D. *undesirable*, chiefly because the trainee will cause the supervisor to worry about possible competition and thus neglect the performance of his duties

13. When discussing lateness with an employee, a supervisor should take the employee to an area where the problem can be discussed privately
    Generally, this practice is considered

    A. *desirable,* chiefly because it gives the employee an opportunity to converse with the supervisor in a very casual way
    B. *desirable,* chiefly because it keeps the problem from being discussed in front of an audience
    C. *undesirable,* chiefly because isolating an employee from his co-workers causes the *rumor-mongers* to spread false gossip about the matter
    D. *undesirable,* chiefly because trivial matters can be mentioned in the open without any repercussions

14. When an officer shows a pattern of abuse in his use of sick leave, a senior officer should

    A. ask the officer for medical proof of all future illnesses
    B. discourage other officers from abusing sick leave by giving the offending officer a public warning
    C. interview the officer and inquire about the reasons for his behavior
    D. acknowledge the officer's right to sick leave as set forth in departmental rules and regulations

15. Of the following, the MAJOR reason why grapevines generally develop in an agency is that

    A. employees have too much idle time
    B. employees want to socialize and gossip with other employees while working
    C. superior officers avoid reporting bad news downward from management to subordinates
    D. there is a communication gap between management and employees

16. If a newly-assigned senior officer is doubtful about the exact details of the assignment he is about to give to an officer, he should GENERALLY

    A. ask to speak to the officer in private and give him another assignment
    B. delay giving the assignment until he clears up his own doubt
    C. attempt to explain to the officer what he knows about the assignment in the best possible way
    D. put the assignment in writing

17. Of the following situations, which one would justify a supervisor's giving direct orders to another supervisor's subordinate?

    A. A supervisor away from his normal assignment observes a serious disturbance and gives orders to the officers in that area.
    B. A supervisor foresees a problem that will arise the next day in another district and immediately proceeds to inform the other supervisor's officers of the action they should take.
    C. A supervisor tells an officer under another supervisor to perform a duty a week from today because he feels it is an urgent matter.
    D. None of the above situations would justify direct supervision by any senior officer.

18. In the planning process, which of the following is NOT a recommended practice in preparing your final plan of action?

    A. Obtain all important available facts related to the problem
    B. Clarify the problem before any plan is created
    C. Make the plan easy to understand so that it can be carried out efficiently
    D. Never make assumptions or forecasts about what could occur

19. Of the following, the BEST way for a senior officer to get his subordinates to carry out his orders is to

    A. explain whenever possible why the orders are being given
    B. let subordinates know in advance the penalties for disobeying his orders
    C. describe the steps that must be followed in performing each order
    D. issue all orders in the form of direct and positive commands

20. It is MOST correct to state that race prejudice is to the GREATEST extent

    A. an inborn human characteristic
    B. the result of training and group association
    C. the product of ghetto areas
    D. a condition limited to adults only

21. *Scapegoating* is a form of prejudice which results MAINLY from

    A. degrading minority groups in an effort to secure status for one's own group
    B. shifting the blame for social inadequacies and ills from oneself to others
    C. thinking of people not as individual persons but rather placing them in carelessly formed, all-embracing classifications
    D. maintaining the existing order to prevent other groups from rising in social and economic status

22. The MOST important step in democratic supervision is

    A. allowing the employee a chance to apologize whenever he makes an error
    B. keeping tight control over employees
    C. making the employee realize that he needs your approval in order to keep his position
    D. showing an interest in the welfare of the employee

23. Evaluating a subordinate's likes and dislikes concerning his work is GENERALLY considered to be

    A. valuable in assigning work details to the subordinate
    B. necessary only when the subordinate complains of dissatisfaction with his daily duties
    C. unnecessary and a waste of time
    D. useful only in establishing a good relationship with the subordinate

24. Employee motivation is very critical in keeping up the morale of employees.
    Of the following, which is generally the BEST method of supervision which both motivates and maintains high morale?

    A. Aid employees in finding satisfaction in their assignments even if it requires extra time and responsibility
    B. Allow employees to work with a free hand and without daily interruptions
    C. Don't get involved or become concerned with interests or problems of employees outside the job
    D. Prove your friendship to a select number of employees so that the remainder of the staff will feel you are a *good guy* to work for

25. When attempting to motivate an experienced individual, it is BEST for a senior officer to appeal to the person's

    A. emotions   B. positive interests
    C. negative feelings   D. inhibitions

KEY (CORRECT ANSWERS)

1. D		11. B	
2. C		12. C	
3. C		13. B	
4. D		14. C	
5. B		15. D	
6. D		16. B	
7. A		17. A	
8. A		18. D	
9. C		19. A	
10. D		20. B	

21. B
22. D
23. A
24. A
25. B

EXAMINATION SECTION
TEST 1

DIRECTIONS: Each question or incomplete statement is followed by several suggested answers or completions. Select the one that BEST answers the question or completes the statement. *PRINT THE LETTER OF THE CORRECT ANSWER IN THE SPACE AT THE RIGHT.*

Questions 1-12.

DIRECTIONS: Questions 1 through 12 are based on the Criminal Procedure Law. Each question consists of two statements. Mark your answer.
    A. if only sentence I is correct
    B. if only sentence II is correct
    C. if sentences I and II are correct
    D. if neither sentence I nor II is correct

1.   I. Except as otherwise provided in the Criminal Procedure Law, a prosecution for a misdemeanor must be commenced within three years after the commission thereof.
  II. Except as otherwise provided in the Criminal Procedure Law, a prosecution for a petty offense must be commenced within two years after the commission thereof.

2.   I. A person may not be prosecuted twice for the same offense.
  II. A defendant may not be convicted of any offense upon the testimony of an accomplice unsupported by corroborative evidence tending to connect the defendant with the commission of such offense.

3.   I. A defendant may testify in his own behalf, but his failure to do so is not a factor from which any inference unfavorable to him may be drawn.
  II. A child less than twelve years old may not testify under oath in a criminal proceeding in a court of law.

4.   I. A person may be convicted of an offense solely upon evidence of a valid confession or admission made by him without additional proof that the offense charged has been committed.
  II. Evidence of a written or oral confession, admission, or other statement made by a defendant with respect to his participation or lack of participation in the offense charged may not be received in evidence against him in a criminal proceeding if such statement was involuntarily made.

5.   I. A summons may be served by a police officer, or by a complainant at least eighteen years of age, or by any other person at least eighteen years old designated by the court.
  II. A summons may be served anywhere in the county of issuance or anywhere in an adjoining county in the state.

6.   I. Any person may arrest another person for a felony anywhere in the state when the latter has in fact committed such felony.
  II. Any person may arrest another person for any offense other than a felony when the latter has in fact committed such offense in his presence, provided that the arrest is made only in the county in which such offense was committed.

7. I. A search warrant must be executed not more than three days after the date and time of issuance and it must thereafter be returned to the court without unnecessary delay.
    II. No search warrant may be executed unless the police officer gives notice of his authority and purpose to the occupant of the premises or vehicle to be searched. In addition, the police officer must serve a copy of the warrant upon the occupant of said premises or vehicle.

8. I. An appearance ticket may be issued by a police officer following an arrest without a warrant if the arrest was for a Class B misdemeanor but not if the arrest was for a Class A misdemeanor.
    II. An appearance ticket may, at the discretion of the police officer or other public servant authorized to issue appearance tickets, be served either personally or by registered or certified mail, return receipt requested.

9. I. Under the *Youthful Offender Treatment* article of the Criminal Procedure Law (Article 720), *youth* means a person charged with a crime who was at least sixteen years old and less than nineteen years old at the time of his alleged commission of such crime.
    II. When an individual has been adjudged eligible for youthful offender treatment, he may be found guilty by reason of a preponderance of the evidence rather than guilty based upon proof beyond a reasonable doubt.

10. I. A police officer may arrest a person without a warrant for any offense, other than for a petty offense, when he has reasonable cause to believe that such person has committed such offense, whether in his presence or otherwise.
    II. A police officer may arrest a person for a petty offense without a warrant when such offense was committed in the officer's presence, within the geographical area of such police officer's employment, and such arrest is made in the county where such offense was committed.

11. I. A police officer may stop a person in a public place located within the geographical area of such officer's employment when he reasonably suspects that such person is committing, has committed or is about to commit either (a) a felony or (b) any misdemeanor as defined in the penal law, and may demand of him his name, address, occupation, the name and address of his employer, and an explanation of his conduct.
    II. Whenever a police officer stops a person in a public place for temporary questioning, he may search such person for a deadly weapon or any instrument, article or substance readily capable of causing serious physical injury and of a sort not ordinarily carried in public places by law-abiding persons.

12. I. A defendant in any criminal action who is less than eighteen years old may refuse to permit himself to be fingerprinted unless accompanied by a parent or legal guardian.
    II. A police officer who is executing an arrest warrant need not have the warrant in his possession; if he has not, he must show it to the defendant upon request as soon after the arrest as possible.

Questions 13-24.

DIRECTIONS: Questions 13 through 24 are to be answered SOLELY on the basis of the Penal Law.

13. A person is guilty of grand larceny in the first degree when he steals property which

    A. consists of personal property valued at more than $1500
    B. is obtained by instilling in the victim a fear that that the victim's membership in a subversive organization will be revealed
    C. consists of goods valued in excess of $250
    D. is obtained by instilling in the victim a fear that an antique vase which he owns will be damaged

14. Using or threatening the immediate use of a dangerous instrument is an element of all of the following offenses EXCEPT _____ in the _____ degree.

    A. robbery; first
    B. burglary; first
    C. robbery; second
    D. burglary; second

15. Which of the following describes a person guilty of escape in the first degree?

    A. A person convicted of a felony escapes from a detention facility.
    B. A person just convicted of a misdemeanor escapes from a courtroom by impersonating a police officer.
    C. A person escapes from a police officer's custody by causing serious physical injury to the officer.
    D. After committing a felony, a person escapes from the scene of the crime by using or threatening the immediate use of a deadly weapon.

16. A person who wantonly and recklessly fires a rifle into a crowd of people without any specific intent to injure or kill would NOT be guilty of

    A. murder if death results
    B. assault in the first degree if serious physical injury results
    C. assault in the second degree if physical injury results
    D. reckless endangerment in the first degree if no injury results

17. Each of the following choices states an offense involving the forcible stealing of property, and certain additional facts.
    In which choice would the defendant be guilty of the offense stated, based SOLELY on the facts given in the choice? Robbery in the

    A. first degree - defendant robs a bank while carrying two sticks of dynamite, which cannot be seen under his jacket
    B. second degree - while defendant and his partner are fleeing from a store they have just robbed, the partner pushes a bystander to the ground, thereby causing a painful bruise to bystander's shoulder
    C. first degree - while robbing a bank, defendant threatens to kidnap and kill the manager's wife unless the manager gives him all the money in the vault
    D. second degree - defendant robs a jewelry store, while his partner waits in a getaway car parked around the corner

18. A person is ALWAYS guilty of a felony if he unlawfully possesses   18.____

    A. any loaded firearm in a vehicle
    B. any deadly weapon and is not a citizen of the United States
    C. any dagger or razor with intent to use the same unlawfully against another
    D. a shotgun in a building used for educational purposes

19. Knowing that Jones intends to rob a bank, Smith gives Jones a rifle to use during the   19.____
    robbery. However, the day before the robbery is supposed to occur, the police arrest
    Jones on an old charge, thereby preventing the robbery.
    Based on these facts, it would be CORRECT to state that Smith is

    A. *not guilty* of any crime
    B. *guilty* of conspiracy in the second degree and criminal facilitation in the second
       degree
    C. *guilty* of criminal facilitation in the second degree but is not guilty of conspiracy in
       the second degree
    D. *guilty* of conspiracy in the second degree but is not guilty of criminal facilitation in
       the second degree

20. Each of the following choices states an offense involving the death of a person, and cer-   20.____
    tain additional facts.
    In which choice would the defendant NOT be guilty of the offense stated, based-
    SOLELY on the facts given in the choice?

    A. Manslaughter in the second degree - when the defendant intentionally causes or
       aids another person to commit suicide
    B. Murder - when the defendant and two other persons attempt to commit escape in
       the second degree, and one of the participants causes the death of a person other
       than one of the participants
    C. Manslaughter in the first degree - when with intent to cause serious physical injury
       to another person, the defendant causes the death of a third person
    D. Murder - when the defendant engages in conduct which creates a grave risk of
       death of another person, and thereby causes the death of another person

21. Which of the following elements would raise the crime of custodial interference from the   21.____
    second degree to the first degree?

    A. The intent to hold a child permanently or for a protracted period
    B. Exposure of the person taken to a risk that his health will be materially impaired
    C. The taking of a child less than sixteen years old from his lawful custodian
    D. Enticement of an incompetent person from lawful custody

22. Which one of the following elements must ALWAYS be present for a person to be guilty of   22.____
    arson in the first degree?

    A. The presence in the building at the time of another person who is not a participant
       in the crime
    B. Intentional damage to a building caused by a fire
    C. Knowledge by the person that another person not a participant in the crime is
       present in the building
    D. Circumstances which render the presence in the building of another person not a
       participant in the crime a reasonable possibility

23. For which of the following crimes is it a necessary element that a person knowingly enter 23.____
or remain unlawfully in a dwelling, as the word *dwelling* is defined in the Penal Law?

    A. Criminal trespass in the first and second degree
    B. Criminal trespass in the second degree and burglary in the first degree
    C. Criminal trespass in the first degree and burglary in the second degree
    D. Burglary in the first and second degree

24. Assume that the police stop a car in which three men are riding. Ward is the driver, and 24.____
Jones and King are passengers. During a lawful search, the police find one-quarter
ounce of morphine concealed in King's coat. Based SOLELY on these facts, it would be
CORRECT to state that

    A. King, Jones, and Ward are all guilty of criminal possession of a dangerous drug
    B. a presumption of knowingly possessing the morphine applies to Ward but not to Jones
    C. King is guilty of criminal possession of a dangerous drug and Ward is guilty of conspiracy
    D. King is guilty of criminal possession of a dangerous drug but Ward and Jones are not

KEY (CORRECT ANSWERS)

1.	D	11.	D
2.	A	12.	B
3.	C	13.	D
4.	B	14.	C
5.	C	15.	A
6.	C	16.	C
7.	D	17.	B
8.	D	18.	A
9.	A	19.	A
10.	C	20.	D

21. B
22. A
23. B
24. D

TEST 2

DIRECTIONS: Each question or incomplete statement is followed by several suggested answers or completions. Select the one that BEST answers the question or completes the statement. *PRINT THE LETTER OF THE CORRECT ANSWER IN THE SPACE AT THE RIGHT.*

1. Which of the following statements is(are) CORRECT? 1.____
 The Criminal Procedure Law (CPL) applies to
 I. all criminal actions and proceedings commenced on or after September 1, 1971, and appeals and other post-judgment proceedings relating thereto.
 II. criminal actions and proceedings commenced before September 1, 1971 but pending thereafter
 III. appeals and other post-judgment proceedings commenced on or after September 1, 1971 which relate to criminal actions and proceedings commenced or concluded prior thereto, provided that, where application of CPL would not be feasible or would work injustice, the former Code of Criminal Procedure shall apply
 IV. criminal procedure matters occurring on or after September 1, 1971 which are not a part of any particular action or case
 The CORRECT answer is:

 A. All of the above B. I *only*
 C. I, II, III D. II, III, IV

2. Which of the following is hearsay? 2.____
 A(n)

 A. written statement by a person not present at the court hearing where the statement is submitted as proof of an occurrence
 B. oral statement in court by a witness of what he saw
 C. written statement of what he saw by a witness present in court
 D. re-enactment by a witness in court of what he saw

3. In a criminal case, a statement by a person not present in court is 3.____

 A. *acceptable* evidence if not objected to by the prosecutor
 B. *acceptable* evidence if not objected to by the defense lawyer
 C. *not acceptable* evidence except in certain well-settled circumstances
 D. *not acceptable* evidence under any circumstances

4. The rule on hearsay is founded on the belief that 4.____

 A. proving someone said an act occurred is not proof that the act did occur
 B. a person who has knowledge about a case should be willing to appear in court
 C. persons not present in court are likely to be unreliable witnesses
 D. permitting persons to testify without appearing in court will lead to a disrespect for law

5. One reason for the general rule that a witness in a criminal case MUST give his testimony in court is that 5.____

 A. a witness may be influenced by threats to make untrue statements
 B. the opposite side is then permitted to question him
 C. the court provides protection for a witness against unfair questioning
 D. the adversary system is designed to prevent a miscarriage of justice.

6. An appeal MAY be taken from a

   A. verdict
   B. judgment
   C. decision
   D. conviction

7. Jury trial commences

   A. with the selection of a jury
   B. when the defendant makes opening address
   C. when the first opening address is made
   D. when the first witness is sworn

8. Adjective criminal law is governed PRIMARILY by the

   A. Penal Law
   B. Civil Practice Law and Rules
   C. Criminal Procedure Law
   D. Code of Criminal Procedure

9. Which of the following contain(s) references included in the definition of *warrant of arrest*?

   I. Process of local criminal court to produce defendant for arraignment
   II. Produce defendant for arraignment upon filed accusatory instrument
   III. Addressed to peace officer to produce defendant for arraignment
   IV. Process of any criminal court requiring defendant to appear before it for arraignment on a prosecutor's information

   The CORRECT answer is:

   A. I, II, III, IV
   B. III *only*
   C. I, II, III
   D. I, II, IV

10. Superior courts have jurisdiction in the following areas:

    I. Unlimited trial jurisdiction of all offenses
    II. Exclusive trial jurisdiction of felonies
    III. Concurrent trial jurisdiction of misdemeanors
    IV. Preliminary jurisdiction of all offenses, exercised only through grand juries

    The CORRECT answer is:

    A. I *only*
    B. I, II
    C. I, II, III
    D. II, III, IV

11. Petty offense means

    A. all violations and traffic infractions
    B. some misdemeanors and all violations
    C. only conduct which is not a traffic infraction and is punishable by imprisonment for not more than 15 days
    D. a class B misdemeanor only

12. An offense committed near a boundary between two adjoining counties of this state may be prosecuted in either of such counties.
    The MAXIMUM distance from a county border is

    A. 1,000 feet   B. 1,000 yards   C. 500 feet   D. 500 yards

13. A felony is committed on the Hudson River south of the northern boundary of New York City.
    The county or counties having jurisdiction to try the case is(are)

    A. New York, Richmond, Bronx, Kings, and Queens Counties
    B. New York, Richmond, and Bronx Counties
    C. New York and Richmond Counties only
    D. New York County only

14. A crime is committed on a bus regularly carrying passengers from Nassau County to Manhattan by way of Queens. At the time of the occurrence, the bus is in Nassau on its way to its terminal point – Manhattan. The victim is a Queens resident. The alleged perpetrator is a resident of Manhattan.
    The county or counties having jurisdiction in this case is(are)

    A. Nassau or New York   B. Nassau or Queens
    C. Nassau, Queens, or Manhattan D. Nassau only

15. Prosecution of a crime MUST be commenced within

    A. one year after commission, for all misdemeanors and petty offenses
    B. two years after commission, for all misdemeanors and petty offenses
    C. 5 years after commission, for all felonies
    D. 5 years after commission, for some felonies

16. A private person in making an arrest is limited as follows:

    A. For an offense, at any hour of day or night
    B. For a crime only, at any hour of any day or night
    C. For a felony only, at any hour of any day or night
    D. All of the above

17. An appearance ticket directs a specific person to appear in a criminal court in connection with the alleged commission of a designated offense.
    This appearance ticket may be issued only by a

    A. local criminal court judge
    B. local criminal court judge or police officer
    C. police officer or authorized public servant
    D. police officer, authorized public servant, or local criminal court judge

18. An arrest by a private person without a warrant can PROPERLY be made in which one of the following situations?

    A. There is reasonable cause to believe that the person being arrested committed a felony.
    B. The person arrested for a felony has in fact committed the felony.
    C. The person arrested for a misdemeanor has in fact committed the misdemeanor.
    D. The person arrested for any offense has in fact committed the offense.

19. A peace officer, outside the geographical area of his employment, has reasonable cause to believe that a felony was committed in his presence.
    In the circumstances,

    A. he may make an arrest, without restriction
    B. he may make an arrest only on the same authority as that of a private person
    C. he may make an arrest during the commission of the felony, immediately thereafter or during immediate flight
    D. none of the above

19.____

20. After making an arrest, a police officer must perform all required recording, fingerprinting, and other related duties.
    He MUST do so

    A. immediately
    B. without unnecessary delay
    C. within 24 hours
    D. within 8 hours

20.____

21. A police officer, acting without a warrant, may arrest a person

    A. only in the geographical area of his employment
    B. outside the geographical area of his employment only for a felony
    C. without restriction, for a petty offense committed anywhere in the state
    D. for a crime committed anywhere in the state

21.____

22. Summons is a process whose SOLE function is to

    A. commence a criminal action
    B. substitute for a warrant of arrest, where a warrant may not be issued
    C. produce defendant for arraignment upon a filed accusatory instrument
    D. inform defendant as to nature of the offenses charged

22.____

23. A summons may be served by

    A. any person without restriction
    B. any person at least 18 years old
    C. a police officer, without restriction
    D. a peace officer, without restriction

23.____

24. An arrest warrant is addressed to and can be executed by

    A. any adult person
    B. a police officer or classification of police officers
    C. a peace officer or classification of peace officers
    D. any person over the age of 18, not a party to the action

24.____

25. Which of the following would invalidate an acknowledgment?

    A. Failure to say deponent is known to notary
    B. Seal is missing
    C. Acts done on Sunday
    D. Affiant misspells his name

25.____

KEY (CORRECT ANSWERS)

1.	A	11.	A
2.	A	12.	D
3.	C	13.	A
4.	A	14.	A
5.	B	15.	D
6.	B	16.	A
7.	A	17.	C
8.	C	18.	B
9.	D	19.	C
10.	D	20.	B

21. D
22. C
23. C
24. B
25. A

TEST 3

DIRECTIONS: Each question or incomplete statement is followed by several suggested answers or completions. Select the one that BEST answers the question or completes the statement. *PRINT THE LETTER OF THE CORRECT ANSWER IN THE SPACE AT THE RIGHT.*

1. A warrant of arrest may be executed anywhere in the state　　　　　　　　　　1.____

    A. without restriction, if it is issued by a city court
    B. in all cases, without restriction
    C. in all cases, provided it is appropriately endorsed by a local criminal court of the county where the arrest is to be made
    D. when issued by the city criminal court

2. A warrant of arrest may be executed on any day　　　　　　　　　　2.____

    A. of the week, at any hour
    B. except Sunday, at any hour of the day; but on Sunday only between 9:00 A.M. and 6:00 P.M.
    C. including Sunday, provided it is so endorsed by the issuing court
    D. except Sunday

3. A police officer or court officer of a criminal court may stop a person, under specified circumstances, when he reasonably suspects that the person is committing, has committed, or is about to commit any felony　　　　　　　　　　3.____

    A. or a Class A misdemeanor defined in the Penal Law
    B. or misdemeanor defined in the Penal Law
    C. or any misdemeanor only
    D. only

4. At a hearing on a felony complaint, defendant　　　　　　　　　　4.____

    A. may testify in his own behalf within the discretion of the court, but he has a right to call witnesses
    B. has a right to testify in his own behalf, but he may call witnesses only within the discretion of the court
    C. has a right to testify in his own behalf and to call witnesses
    D. may testify in his own behalf, within the discretion of the court, and call witnesses in his behalf, within the discretion of the court

5. A grand jury, to be legally constituted, MUST consist of _____ members.　　　　5.____

    A. not less than 16 and not more than 23
    B. not less than 12 and not more than 16
    C. not less than 12 and not more than 23
    D. at least 12

6. At a preliminary hearing on a felony complaint,　　　　　　　　　　6.____
    I. the defendant must be present
    II. the defendant has a right to be present, but he may waive this right
    III. the defendant has a right to call witnesses in his behalf
    IV. all witnesses called may be cross-examined

The CORRECT answer is:

A. I, II   B. II, III   C. I, IV   D. II, IV

7. The number and term of grand juries empanelled for a court are determined generally by   7.____

    A. Supreme Court in the county, on application of the District Attorney showing the estimated need
    B. Rules of the court for which the grand jury is drawn
    C. Judicial Conference regulations
    D. Appellate Division rules

8. The quantum of proof required for a court to hold a defendant for grand jury action on a felony complaint is proof   8.____

    A. affording the court reasonable cause to believe
    B. sufficient for a reasonable man
    C. by a fair preponderance of the evidence
    D. beyond a reasonable doubt

9. The acting foreman of a grand jury is   9.____

    A. chosen by lot
    B. chosen by the court
    C. the second grand juror to be empanelled
    D. chosen by the grand jurors

10. When a grand jury requires legal advice, they may receive it   10.____

    A. only from the court, District Attorney, or an attorney designated by either
    B. either from the court or District Attorney, only
    C. only from the District Attorney
    D. only from the court

11. In all cases, when a motion is made for a change of venue, a(n)   11.____

    A. application for a stay, denied by a Supreme Court justice, may not thereafter be granted by a justice of the Appellate Division
    B. application for a stay, denied by a Supreme Court justice, may be reviewed and granted by a justice of the Appellate Division
    C. stay may be granted only by any Supreme Court justice in the judicial district
    D. stay may be granted by any superior court judge in the judicial district

12. Evidence of mental disease or defect as a trial defense excluding criminal responsibility is admissible   12.____

    A. only as to a defendant who has previously been examined under court order by two qualified psychiatrists
    B. provided the defendant has served and filed timely written notice of intention to rely thereon
    C. provided the People have served a demand on the defendant to give notice of this defense
    D. in all cases without restriction

13. On a defense of alibi,

    A. the People in all cases are entitled on trial to an adjournment not in excess of 3 days
    B. a court may receive testimony as in D below but on application must grant an adjournment of not less than 7 days
    C. a court may not receive testimony as in D below
    D. a court may receive testimony, in its discretion, from a witness who was not included in defendant's notice of alibi

14. Which of the following statements are CORRECT?
    I. The People, having the burden of proof, address the jury before defendant at all stages.
    II. A closing address to the jury by the prosecution is required.
    III. A closing address to the jury by both sides is discretionary.
    IV. An opening address to the jury by both sides is discretionary.
    V. The People in all cases must make an opening address to the jury.

    The CORRECT answer is:

    A. I, II, III
    B. II, III, IV
    C. I, II, IV
    D. I, II, V

15. In selecting a jury, the MAXIMUM total number of challenges to alternate jurors that may be exercised by BOTH parties is

    A. 16
    B. 8
    C. 4
    D. 2

16. A grand jury witness may be called only on request of the

    A. court, District Attorney, or grand jury
    B. court
    C. District Attorney or the grand jury
    D. grand jury

17. A prospective defendant in a grand jury proceeding who wishes the grand jury to hear a witness in his behalf is limited by the fact that

    A. the grand jury, in its discretion, may hear the witness if the defendant makes an oral or written request
    B. the grand jury must hear the witness if the defendant makes an oral or written request
    C. the grand jury must hear the witness only if the defendant makes a written request
    D. there may be no legal basis for such a request

18. When a charge has been dismissed by a grand jury following its consideration of the matter, which of the following is CORRECT?

    A. It may be resubmitted to successive grand juries by court order, without limitation.
    B. It may be resubmitted to a grand jury if a court so authorizes, but no further submission thereafter is permissible.
    C. Without court order, it may be considered by another grand jury, but not by the same grand jury.
    D. It may again be considered by the same grand jury, without court order.

19. An indictment MUST contain
    I. endorsement, *A True Bill,* signed by the district attorney
    II. applicable section number of the statute allegedly violated
    III. date or period when alleged conduct occurred
    IV. statement in each court that the grand jury accuses the defendant of a designated offense

    The CORRECT answer is:

    A. I, II, IV
    B. III, IV
    C. II, III, IV
    D. I, II, III, IV

20. With respect to an offense raised to higher grade by reason solely of a previous conviction, which of the following statements is CORRECT?

    A. Under no circumstances is a jury permitted to know of the previous conviction.
    B. The order of trial is in this instance substantially the same as in other cases, except for arraignment on a special information.
    C. Before any proceeding to establish defendant's identity and previous conviction, he must be advised of the privilege against self-incrimination.
    D. The defendant's conviction of the predicate case may be established at any time before the case goes to the jury.

21. The term *petty offense* includes

    A. no misdemeanors, some violations, all traffic infractions
    B. no misdemeanors, but all violations and traffic infractions
    C. some misdemeanors, all violations and traffic infractions
    D. all misdemeanors, violations, and traffic infractions

22. Conviction, as defined in CPL, means

    A. entry of guilty plea, or guilty verdict
    B. serving of sentence
    C. entry of final judgment
    D. imposition and entry of sentence

23. With regard to a non-jury trial, which of the following is CORRECT?

    A. Trial commences when both parties appear, are ready, and the court announces that the case is on trial. The court's determination as to guilt or innocence is properly termed a verdict.
    B. If there is no opening address, trial commences when the first witness is sworn, and the court's determination as to guilt or innocence is properly termed a verdict.
    C. An opening address, if made, commences the trial, and the court's determination of guilt or innocence is properly termed a decision.
    D. There must be an opening address to the court; this commences the trial; and the court's determination of guilt or innocence is properly termed a decision.

24. In relation to double jeopardy, a person may not be twice prosecuted for the same offense.
    Assuming the same offense, which of the following does NOT relate to double jeopardy under CPL?

A. Defendant is found not guilty after trial in one jurisdiction
B. An accusatory instrument is filed in a court of another country
C. An accusatory instrument is filed in a Federal court
D. An accusatory instrument is filed in a state other than New York

25. Which of the following is NOT applicable to a warrant of arrest? 25.____

   A. Its function is to produce defendant for arraignment.
   B. It commences a criminal action.
   C. It is issued only by a local criminal court.
   D. It is addressed to a police officer.

KEY (CORRECT ANSWERS)

1. D
2. A
3. A
4. B
5. A

6. D
7. D
8. A
9. B
10. B

11. A
12. B
13. D
14. D
15. A

16. C
17. A
18. B
19. B
20. B

21. B
22. A
23. B
24. B
25. B

READING COMPREHENSION
UNDERSTANDING AND INTERPRETING WRITTEN MATERIAL
EXAMINATION SECTION
TEST 1

DIRECTIONS: Each question or incomplete statement is followed by several suggested answers or completions. Select the one that BEST answers the question or completes the statement. *PRINT THE LETTER OF THE CORRECT ANSWER IN THE SPACE AT THE RIGHT.*

Questions 1-4.

DIRECTIONS: Questions 1 through 4 are to be answered SOLELY on the basis of the following passage.

Those engaged in the exercise of First Amendment rights by pickets, marches, parades, and open-air assemblies are not exempted from obeying valid local traffic ordinances. In a recent pronouncement, Mr. Justice Baxter, speaking for the Supreme Court, wrote:

The rights of free speech and assembly, while fundamental to our democratic society, still do not mean that everyone with opinions or beliefs to express may address a group at any public place and at any time. The constitutional guarantee of liberty implies the existence of an organized society maintaining public order, without which liberty itself would be lost in the excesses of anarchy. The control of travel on the streets is a clear example of governmental responsibility to insure this necessary order. A restriction in that relation, designed to promote the public convenience in the interest of all, and not susceptible to abuses of discriminatory application, cannot be disregarded by the attempted exercise of some civil rights which, in other circumstances, would be entitled to protection. One would not be justified in ignoring the familiar red light because this was thought to be a means of social protest. Governmental authorities have the duty and responsibility to keep their streets open and available for movement. A group of demonstrators could not insist upon the right to cordon off a street, or entrance to a public or private building, and allow no one to pass who did not agree to listen to their exhortations.

1. Which of the following statements BEST reflects Mr. Justice Baxter's view of the relationship between liberty and public order?

    A. Public order cannot exist without liberty.
    B. Liberty cannot exist without public order.
    C. The existence of liberty undermines the existence of public order.
    D. The maintenance of public order insures the existence of liberty.

1.____

2. According to the above passage, local traffic ordinances result from

    A. governmental limitations on individual liberty
    B. governmental responsibility to insure public order
    C. majority rule as determined by democratic procedures
    D. restrictions on expression of dissent

2.____

3. The above passage suggests that government would be acting improperly if a local traffic ordinance

   A. was enforced in a discriminatory manner
   B. resulted in public inconvenience
   C. violated the right of free speech and assembly
   D. was not essential to public order

4. Of the following, the MOST appropriate title for the above passage is

   A. THE RIGHTS OF FREE SPEECH AND ASSEMBLY
   B. ENFORCEMENT OF LOCAL TRAFFIC ORDINANCES
   C. FIRST AMENDMENT RIGHTS AND LOCAL TRAFFIC ORDINANCES
   D. LIBERTY AND ANARCHY

Questions 5-8

DIRECTIONS: Questions 5 through 8 are to be answered SOLELY on the basis of the following passage

On November 8, 1976, the Supreme Court refused to block the payment of Medicaid funds for elective abortions. The Court's action means that a new Federal statute that bars the use of Federal funds for abortions unless abortion is necessary to save the life of the mother will not go into effect for many months, if at all.

A Federal District Court in Brooklyn ruled the following month that the statute was unconstitutional and ordered that Federal reimbursement for the costs of abortions continue on the same basis as reimbursements for the costs of pregnancy and childbirth-related services.

Technically, what the Court did today was to deny a request by Senator Howard Ramsdell and others for a stay blocking enforcement of the District Court order pending appeal. The Court's action was a victory for New York City. The City's Health and Hospitals Corporation initiated one of the two lawsuits challenging the new statute that led to the District Court's decision. The Corporation also opposed the request for a Supreme Court stay of that decision, telling the Court in a memorandum that a stay would subject the Corporation to a *grave and irreparable injury.*

5. According to the above passage, it would be CORRECT to state that the Health and Hospitals Corporation

   A. joined Senator Ramsdell in his request for a stay
   B. opposed the statute which limited reimbursement for the cost of abortions
   C. claimed that it would experience a loss if the District Court order was enforced
   D. appealed the District Court decision

6. The above passage indicates that the Supreme Court acted in DIRECT response to

   A. a lawsuit initiated by the Health and Hospitals Corporation
   B. a ruling by a Federal District Court
   C. a request for a stay
   D. the passage of a new Federal statute

7. According to the above passage, it would be CORRECT to state that the Supreme Court

   A. blocked enforcement of the District Court order
   B. refused a request for a stay to block enforcement of the Federal statute
   C. ruled that the new Federal statute was unconstitutional
   D. permitted payment of Federal funds for abortion to continue

8. Following are three statements concerning abortion that might be correct:
   I. Abortion costs are no longer to be Federally reimbursed on the same basis as those for pregnancy and childbirth
   II. Federal funds have not been available for abortions except to save the life of the mother
   III. Medicaid has paid for elective abortions in the past

   According to the passage above, which of the following CORRECTLY classifies the above statements into those that are true and those that are not true?

   A. I is true, but II and III are not.
   B. I and III are true, but II is not.
   C. I and II are true, but III is not.
   D. III is true, but I and II are not.

Questions 9-12.

DIRECTIONS: Questions 9 through 12 are to be answered SOLELY on the basis of the following passage.

A person may use physical force upon another person when and to the extent he reasonably believes such to be necessary to defend himself or a third person from what he reasonably believes to be the use or imminent use of unlawful physical force by such other person, unless (a) the latter's conduct was provoked by the actor himself with intent to cause physical injury to another person; or (b) the actor was the initial aggressor; or (c) the physical force involved is the product of a combat by agreement not specifically authorized by law.

A person may not use deadly physical force upon another person under the circumstances specified above unless (a) he reasonably believes that such other person is using or is about to use deadly physical force. Even in such case, however, the actor may not use deadly physical force if he knows he can, with complete safety, as to himself and others avoid the necessity of doing so by retreating; except that he is under no duty to retreat if he is in his dwelling and is not the initial aggressor; or (b) he reasonably believes that such other person is committing or attempting to commit a kidnapping, forcible rape, or forcible sodomy.

9. Jones and Smith, who have not met before, get into an argument in a tavern. Smith takes a punch at Jones, but misses. Jones then hits Smith on the chin with his fist. Smith falls to the floor and suffers minor injuries.
   According to the above passage, it would be CORRECT to state that _____ justified in using physical force.

   A. only Smith was
   B. only Jones was
   C. both Smith and Jones were
   D. neither Smith nor Jones was

10. While walking down the street, Brady observes Miller striking Mrs. Adams on the head with his fist in an attempt to steal her purse.
According to the above passage, it would be CORRECT to state that Brady would

   A. not be justified in using deadly physical force against Miller since Brady can safely retreat
   B. be justified in using physical force against Miller but not deadly physical force
   C. not be justified in using physical force against Miller since Brady himself is not being attacked
   D. be justified in using deadly physical force

11. Winters is attacked from behind by Sharp, who attempts to beat up Winters with a blackjack. Winters disarms Sharp and succeeds in subduing him with a series of blows to the head. Sharp stops fighting and explains that he thought Winters was the person who had robbed his apartment a few minutes before, but now realizes his mistake.
According to the above passage, it would be CORRECT to state that

   A. Winters was justified in using physical force on Sharp only to the extent necessary to defend himself
   B. Winters was not justified in using physical force on Sharp since Sharp's attack was provoked by what he believed to be Winters' behavior
   C. Sharp was justified in using physical force on Winters since he reasonably believed that Winters had unlawfully robbed him
   D. Winters was justified in using physical force on Sharp only because Sharp was acting mistakenly in attacking him

12. Roberts hears a noise in the cellar of his home, and, upon investigation, discovers an intruder, Welch. Welch moves towards Roberts in a threatening manner, thrusts his hand into a bulging pocket, and withdraws what appears to be a gun. Roberts thereupon strikes Welch over the head with a golf club. He then sees that the *gun* is a toy. Welch later dies of head injuries. According to the above passage, it would be CORRECT to state that Roberts was

   A. justified in using deadly physical force because he reasonably believed Welch was about to use deadly physical force
   B. not justified in using deadly physical force
   C. justified in using deadly physical force only because he did not provoke Welch's conduct
   D. justified in using deadly physical force only because he was not the initial aggressor

Questions 13-16.

DIRECTIONS: Questions 13 through 16 are to be answered SOLELY on the basis of the following passage.

From the beginning, the Supreme Court has supervised the fairness of trials conducted by the Federal government. But the Constitution, as originally drafted, gave the court no such general authority in state cases. The court's power to deal with state cases comes from the Fourteenth Amendment, which became part of the Constitution in 1868. The crucial provision forbids any state to *deprive any person of life, liberty, or property without due process of law.*

The guarantee of *due process* would seem, at the least, to require fair procedure in criminal trials. But curiously the Supreme Court did not speak on the question for many decades. During that time, however, the due process clause was interpreted to bar *unreasonable* state economic regulations, such as minimum wage laws.

In 1915, there came the case of Leo M. Frank, a Georgian convicted of murder in a trial that he contended was dominated by mob hysteria. Historians now agree that there was such hysteria, with overtones of anti-semitism.

The Supreme Court held that it could not look past the findings of the Georgia courts that there had been no mob atmosphere at the trial. Justices Oliver Wendell Holmes and Charles Evans Hughes dissented, arguing that the constitutional guarantee would be *a barren one* if the Federal courts could not make their own inferences from the facts.

In 1923, the case of Moore v. Dempsey involved five Arkansas Blacks convicted of murder and sentenced to death in a community so aroused against them that at one point they were saved from lynching only by Federal troops. Witnesses against them were said to have been beaten into testifying.

The court, though not actually setting aside the convictions, directed a lower Federal court to hold a habeas corpus hearing to find out whether the trial had been fair, or whether the whole proceeding had been *a mask—that counsel, jury, and judge were swept to the fatal end by an irresistible wave of public passion.*

13. According to the above passage, the Supreme Court's INITIAL interpretation of the Fourteenth Amendment

    A. protected state supremacy in economic matters
    B. increased the scope of Federal jurisdiction
    C. required fair procedures in criminal trials
    D. prohibited the enactment of minimum wage laws

14. According to the above passage, the Supreme Court in the Frank case

    A. denied that there had been mob hysteria at the trial
    B. decided that the guilty verdict was supported by the evidence
    C. declined to question the state court's determination of the facts
    D. found that Leo Frank had not received *due process*

15. According to the above passage, the dissenting judges in the Frank case maintained that

    A. due process was an empty promise in the circumstances of that case
    B. the Federal courts could not guarantee certain provisions of the Constitution
    C. the Federal courts should not make their own inferences from the facts in state cases
    D. the Supreme Court had rendered the Constitution *barren*

16. Of the following, the MOST appropriate title for the above passage is 16.____
    A. THE CONDUCT OF FEDERAL TRIALS
    B. THE DEVELOPMENT OF STATES' RIGHTS: 1868-1923
    C. MOORE V. DEMPSEY: A CASE STUDY IN CRIMINAL JUSTICE
    D. DUE PROCESS-THE EVOLUTION OF A CONSTITUTIONAL CORNERSTONE

Questions 17-20.

DIRECTIONS: Questions 17 through 20 are to be answered SOLELY on the basis of the following passage.

The difficulty experienced in determining which party has the burden of proving payment or non-payment is due largely to a lack of consistency between the rules of pleading and the rules of proof. In some cases, a plaintiff is obligated by a rule of pleading to allege non-payment on his complaint, yet is not obligated to prove non-payment on the trial. An action upon a contract for the payment of money will serve as an illustration. In such a case, the plaintiff must allege non-payment in his complaint, but the burden of proving payment on the trial is upon the defendant. An important and frequently cited case on this problem is Conkling v. Weatherwax. In that case, the action was brought to establish and enforce a legacy as a lien upon real property. The defendant alleged in her answer that the legacy had been paid. There was no witness competent to testify for the plaintiff to show that the legacy had not been paid. Therefore, the question of the burden of proof became of primary importance since, if the plaintiff had the burden of proving non-payment, she must fail in her action; whereas if the burden of proof was on the defendant to prove payment, the plaintiff might win. The Court of Appeals held that the burden of proof was on the plaintiff. In the course of his opinion, Judge Vann attempted to harmonize the conflicting cases on this subject, and for that purpose formulated three rules. These rules have been construed and applied to numerous subsequent cases. As so construed and applied, these may be summarized as follows:

Rule 1. In an action upon a contract for the payment of money only, where the complaint does not allege a balance due over and above all payments made, the plaintiff must allege nonpayment in his complaint, but the burden of proving payment is upon the defendant. In such a case, payment is an affirmative defense which the defendant must plead in his answer. If the defendant fails to plead payment, but pleads a general denial instead, he will not be permitted to introduce evidence of payment.

Rule 2. Where the complaint sets forth a balance in excess of all payments, owing to the structure of the pleading, burden is upon the plaintiff to prove his allegation. In this case, the defendant is not required to plead payment as a defense in his answer but may introduce evidence of payment under a general denial.

Rule 3. When the action is not upon contract for the payment of money, but is upon an obligation created by operation of law, or is for the enforcement of a lien where non-payment of the amount secured is part of the cause of action, it is necessary both to allege and prove the fact of nonpayment.

17. In the above passage, the case of Conkling v. Weatherwax was cited PRIMARILY to illustrate   17.____

    A. a case where the burden of proof was on the defendant to prove payment
    B. how the question of the burden of proof can affect the outcome of a case
    C. the effect of a legacy as a lien upon real property
    D. how conflicting cases concerning the burden of proof were harmonized

18. According to the above passage, the pleading of payment is a defense in Rule(s)   18.____

    A. 1, but not Rules 2 and 3
    B. 2, but not Rules 1 and 3
    C. 1 and 3, but not Rule 2
    D. 2 and 3, but not Rule 1

19. The facts in Conkling v. Weatherwax CLOSELY resemble the conditions described in   19.____

    A. Rule #1
    B. Rule #2
    C. Rule #3
    D. none of the rules

20. The MAJOR topic of the above passage may BEST be described as   20.____

    A. determining the ownership of property
    B. providing a legal definition
    C. placing the burden of proof
    D. formulating rules for deciding cases

Questions 21-25.

DIRECTIONS: Questions 21 through 25 are to be answered SOLELY on the basis of the following passage.

The law is quite clear that evidence obtained in violation of Section 605 of the Federal Communications Act is not admissible in Federal court. However, the law as to the admissibility of evidence in state court is far from clear. Had the Supreme Court of the United States made the wiretap exclusionary rule applicable to the states, such confusion would not exist.

In the case of Alton v. Texas, the Supreme Court was called upon to determine whether wiretapping by state and local officers came within the proscription of the Federal statute and, if so, whether Section 605 required the same remedies for its vindication in state courts. In answer to the first question, Mr. Justice Minton, speaking for the court, flatly stated that Section 605 made it a federal crime for anyone to intercept telephone messages and divulge what he learned. The court went on to say that a state officer who testified in state court concerning the existence, contents, substance, purport, effect, or meaning of an intercepted conversation violated the Federal law and committed a criminal act. In regard to the second question, how-ever, the Supreme Court felt constrained by due regard for federal-state relations to answer in the negative. Mr. Justice Minton stated that the court would not presume, in the absence of a clear manifestation of congressional intent, that Congress intended to supersede state rules of evidence.

Because the Supreme Court refused to apply the exclusionary rule to wiretap evidence that was being used in state courts, the states respectively made this decision for themselves. According to hearings held before a congressional committee in 1975, six states authorize wiretapping by statute, 33 states impose total bans on wiretapping, and 11 states have no definite statute on the subject. For examples of extremes, a statute in Pennsylvania will be compared with a statute in New York.

The Pennsylvania statute provides that no communications by telephone or telegraph can be intercepted without permission of both parties. It also specifically prohibits such interception by public officials and provides that evidence obtained cannot be used in court.

The lawmakers in New York, recognizing the need for legal wire-tapping, authorized wiretapping by statute. A New York law authorizes the issuance of an ex parte order upon oath or affirmation for limited wiretapping. The aim of the New York law is to allow court-ordered wiretapping and to encourage the testimony of state officers concerning such wiretapping in court. The New York law was found to be constitutional by the New York State Supreme Court in 1975. Other states, including Oregon, Maryland, Nevada, and Massachusetts, enacted similar laws which authorize court-ordered wiretapping.

To add to this legal disarray, the vast majority of the states, including New Jersey and New York, permit wiretapping evidence to be received in court even though obtained in violation of the state laws and of Section 605 of the Federal act. However, some states, such as Rhode Island, have enacted statutory exclusionary rules which provide that illegally procured wiretap evidence is incompetent in civil as well as criminal actions.

21. According to the above passage, a state officer who testifies in New York State court concerning the contents of a conversation he overheard through a court-ordered wire-tap is in violation of _____ law.

    A. state law but not federal
    B. federal law but not state
    C. federal law and state
    D. neither federal nor state

22. According to the above passage, which of the following statements concerning states statutes on wiretapping is CORRECT?

    A. The number of states that impose total bans on wiretapping is three times as great as the number of states with no definite statute on wiretapping.
    B. The number of states having no definite statute on wiretapping is more than twice the number of states authorizing wiretapping.
    C. The number of states which authorize wiretapping by statute and the number of states having no definite statute on wiretapping exceed the number of states imposing total bans on wiretapping.
    D. More states authorize wiretapping by statute than impose total bans on wiretapping.

23. Following are three statements concerning wiretapping that might be valid: 23.____
    I. In Pennsylvania, only public officials may legally intercept telephone communications.
    II. In Rhode Island, evidence obtained through an illegal wiretap is incompetent in criminal, but not civil, actions.
    III. Neither Massachusetts nor Pennsylvania authorizes wiretapping by public officials.

    According to the above passage, which of the following CORRECTLY classifies these statements into those that are valid and those that are not?

    A. I is valid, but II and III are not.
    B. II is valid, but I and III are not.
    C. II and III are valid, but I is not.
    D. None of the statements is valid.

24. According to the above passage, evidence obtained in violation of Section 605 of the Federal Communications Act is inadmissible in 24.____

    A. federal court but not in any state courts
    B. federal court and all state courts
    C. all state courts but not in federal court
    D. federal court and some state courts

25. In regard to state rules of evidence, Mr. Justice Minton expressed the Court's opinion that Congress 25.____

    A. intended to supersede state rules of evidence, as manifested by Section 605 of the Federal Communications Act
    B. assumed that federal statutes would govern state rules of evidence in all wiretap cases
    C. left unclear whether it intended to supersede state rules of evidence
    D. precluded itself from superseding state rules of evidence through its regard for federal-state relations

KEY (CORRECT ANSWERS)

1. B
2. B
3. A
4. C
5. B

6. C
7. D
8. D
9. B
10. B

11. A
12. A
13. D
14. C
15. A

16. D
17. B
18. A
19. C
20. C

21. B
22. A
23. D
24. D
25. C

TEST 2

DIRECTIONS: Each question or incomplete statement is followed by several suggested answers or completions. Select the one that BEST answers the question or completes the Statement. *PRINT THE LETTER OF THE CORRECT ANSWER IN THE SPACE AT THE RIGHT.*

Questions 1-3.

DIRECTIONS: Questions 1 through 3 are to be answered SOLELY on the basis of the following passage.

The State Assembly has passed a bill that would require all state agencies, public authorities, and local governments to refuse bids in excess of $2,000 from any foreign firm or corporation. The only exceptions to this outright prohibition against public buying of foreign goods or services would be for products not available in this country, goods of a quality unobtainable from an American supplier, and products using foreign materials that are *substantially* manufactured in the United States.

This bill is a flagrant violation of the United States' officially espoused trade principles. It would add to the costs of state and local governments. It could provoke retaliatory action from many foreign governments against the state and other American producers, and foreign governments would be fully entitled to take such retaliatory action under the General Agreement on Tariffs and Trade, which the United States has signed.

The State Senate, which now has the Assembly bill before it, should reject this protectionist legislation out of enlightened regard for the interests of the taxpayers and producers of the State—as well as for those of the nation and its trading partners generally. In this time of unemployment and international monetary disorder, the State—with its reputation for intelligent and progressive law-making—should avoid contributing to what could become a tidal wave of protectionism here and overseas.

1. Under the requirements of the bill passed by the State Assembly, a bid from a foreign manufacturer in excess of $2,000 can be accepted by a state agency or local government only if it meets which one of the following requirements?
The

   A. bid is approved individually by the State Legislature
   B. bidder is willing to accept payment in United States currency
   C. bid is for an item of a quality unobtainable from an American supplier
   D. bid is for an item which would be more expensive if it were purchased from an American supplier

2. The author of the above passage feels that the bill passed by the State Assembly should be

   A. passed by the State Senate and put into effect
   B. passed by the State Senate but vetoed by the Governor
   C. reintroduced into the State Assembly and rejected
   D. rejected by the State Senate

3. The author of the above passage calls the practice of prohibiting purchase of products manufactured by foreign countries

   A. prohibition
   B. protectionism
   C. retaliatory action
   D. isolationism

Questions 4-7.

DIRECTIONS: Questions 4 through 7 are to be answered SOLELY on the basis of the following passage.

   Data processing is by no means a new invention. In one form or another, it has been carried on throughout the entire history of civilization. In its most general sense, data processing means organizing data so that it can be used for a specific purpose-a procedure commonly known simply as *record-keeping* or *paperwork*. With the development of modern office equipment, and particularly with the recent introduction of computers, the techniques of data processing have become highly elaborate and sophisticated, but the basic purpose remains the same: Turning raw data into useful information.

   The key concept here is usefulness. The data, or input, that is to be processed can be compared to the raw material that is to go into a manufacturing process. The information, or output, that results from data processing—like the finished product of a manufacturer—should be clearly usable. A collection of data has little value unless it is converted into information that serves a specific function.

4. The expression *paperwork,* as it is used in this passage,

   A. shows that the author regards such operations as a waste of time
   B. has the same general meaning as *data processing*
   C. refers to methods of record-keeping that are no longer in use
   D. indicates that the public does not understand the purpose of data processing

5. The above passage indicates that the use of computers has

   A. greatly simplified the clerical work in an office
   B. led to more complicated systems for the handling of data
   C. had no effect whatsoever on data processing
   D. made other modern office machines obsolete

6. Which of the following BEST expresses the basic principle of data processing as it is described in the above passage?

   A. Input-processing-output
   B. Historical record-keeping-modern techniques -specific functions
   C. Office equipment-computer-accurate data
   D. Raw material-manufacturer-retailer

7. According to the above passage, data processing may be described as

   A. a new management technique
   B. computer technology
   C. information output
   D. record-keeping

Questions 8-10.

DIRECTIONS: Questions 8 through 10 are to be answered SOLELY on the basis of the following passage.

A loan receipt is an instrument devised to permit the insurance company to bring an action against the wrongdoer in the name of the insured despite the fact that the insured no longer has any financial interest in the outcome. It provides, in effect, that the amount of the loss is advanced to the insured as a loan which is repayable only up to the extent of any recovery made from the wrongdoer. The insured further agrees to enter and prosecute suit against the wrongdoer in his own name. Such a receipt substitutes a loan for a payment for the purpose of permitting the insurance company to press its action against the wrongdoer in the name of the insured.

8. According to the above passage, the purpose behind the use of a loan receipt is to   8.____

   A. guarantee that the insurance company gets repayment from the person insured
   B. insure repayment of all expenditures to the named insured
   C. make it possible for the insurance company to sue in the name of the policyowner
   D. prevent the wrongdoer from escaping the natural consequences of his act

9. According to the above passage, the amount of the loan which must be paid back to the   9.____
   insurance company equals but does NOT exceed the amount

   A. of the loss
   B. on the face of the policy
   C. paid to the insured
   D. recovered from the wrongdoer

10. According to the above passage, by giving a loan receipt, the person insured agrees to   10.____

    A. a suit against the wrongdoer in his own name
    B. forego any financial gain from the outcome of the suit
    C. institute an action on behalf of the insurance company
    D. repay the insurance company for the loan received

Questions 11-12.

DIRECTIONS: Questions 11 and 12 are to be answered SOLELY on the basis of the following passage.

Open air markets originally came into existence spontaneously when groups of pushcart peddlers congregated in spots where business was good. Good business induced them to return to these spots daily and, thus, unofficial open air markets arose. These peddlers paid no fees, and the city received no revenue from them. Confusion and disorder reigned in these unsupervised markets; the earliest arrivals secured the best locations, unless or until forcibly ejected by stronger or tougher peddlers. Although the open air markets supplied a definite need in the community, there were many detrimental factors involved in their operation. They were unsightly, created unsanitary conditions in market streets by the deposit of garbage and waste and were a definite obstruction to traffic, as well as a fire hazard.

11. On the basis of the above passage, the MOST accurate of the following statements is:

    A. Each peddler in the original open air markets had his own fixed location.
    B. Open air markets were originally organized by means of agreements between groups of pushcart peddlers.
    C. The locations of these markets depended upon the amount of business the vendors were able to do.
    D. There was confusion and disorder in these open air markets because the peddlers were not required to pay any fees to the city.

12. Of the following, the MOST valid implication which can be made on the basis of the above passage is that the

    A. detrimental aspect of the operations of open air markets was the probable reason for the creation of enclosed markets under the supervision of the Department of Markets
    B. open air markets could not supply any community need without proper supervision
    C. original open air markets were good examples of the operation of fair competition in business
    D. possibility of obtaining a source of revenue was probably the most important reason for the city's ultimate undertaking of the supervision of open air markets

Questions 13-14.

DIRECTIONS: Questions 13 and 14 are to be answered SOLELY on the basis of the following passage.

  A person who displays on his window, door, or in his place of business words or letters in Hebraic characters other than the word *kosher,* or any sign, emblem, insignia, six-pointed star, symbol or mark in simulation of same, without displaying in conjunction there-with in English letters of at least the same size as such characters, signs, emblems, insignia or marks, the words *we sell kosher meat and food only* or *we sell non-kosher meat and food only* or *we sell both kosher and non-kosher meat and food,* as the case may be, is guilty of a misdemeanor. Possession of non-kosher meat and food in any place of business advertising the sale of kosher meat and food only is presumptive evidence that the person in possession exposes the same for sale with intent to defraud, in violation of the provisions of this section.

13. Of the following, the MOST valid implication that can be made on the basis of the above passage is that a person who

    A. displays on his window a six-pointed star in addition to the word *kosher* in Hebraic letters is guilty of intent to defraud
    B. displays on his window the word *kosher* in Hebraic characters intends to indicate that he has only kosher food for sale
    C. sells both kosher and non-kosher food in the same place of business is guilty of a misdemeanor
    D. sells only that type of food which can be characterized as neither kosher nor non-kosher, such as fruit and vegetables, without an explanatory sign in English is guilty of intent to defraud

14. Of the following, the one which would constitute a violation of the rules of the above passage is a case in which a person 14.____

    A. displays the word *kosher* on his window in Hebraic letters has only kosher meat and food in the store but has some non-kosher meat in the rear of the establishment
    B. selling both kosher and non-kosher meat and food uses words in Hebraic letters, other than the word *kosher,* on his window and a sign of the same size letters in English stating *we sell both kosher and non-kosher meat and food*
    C. selling only kosher meat and food uses words in Hebraic letters, other than the word *kosher,* on his window and a sign of the same size letters in English stating *we sell kosher meat and food only*
    D. selling only non-kosher meat and food displays a six-pointed star on his window and a sign of the same size letters in English stating *we sell only non-kosher meat and food*

Questions 15-16.

DIRECTIONS: Questions 15 and 16 are to be answered SOLELY on the basis of the following passage.

COMMODITIES IN GLASS BOTTLES OR JARS

The contents of the bottle may be stated in terms of weight or of fluid measure, the weight being indicated in terms of pounds and ounces and the fluid measure being indicated in terms of gallons, quarts, pints, half-pints, gills, or fluid ounces. When contents are liquid, the amount should not be stated in terms of weight. The marking indicating content is to be on a tag attached to the bottle or upon a label. The letters shall be in bold-faced type at least one-ninth of an inch (1/9") in height for bottles or jars having a capacity of a gill, half-pint, pint, or multiples of a pint, and letters at least three-sixteenths of an inch (3/16") in height for bottles of other capacities, on a part of the tag or label free from other printing or ornamentation, leaving a clear space around the marking which indicates the contents.

15. Of the following, the one which does NOT meet the requirements of the above passage is a 15.____

    A. bottle of cooking oil with a label stating *contents—16 fluid ounces* in appropriate sized letters
    B. bottle of vinegar with a label stating *contents—8 ounces avoir.* in appropriate sized letters
    C. glass jar filled with instant coffee with a label stating *contents—1 lb. 3 ozs. avoir.* in appropriate sized letters
    D. glass jar filled with liquid bleach with a label stating *contents—1 quart* in appropriate sized letters

16. Of the following, the one which does meet the requirements of the above passage is a 16.____

    A. bottle filled with a low-calorie liquid sweetener with a label stating *contents—3 fluid ounces* in letters 1/12" high
    B. bottle filled with ammonia solution for cleaning with a label stating *contents—1 pint* in letters 1/10" high

C. jar filled with baking powder with a label stating *contents—$\frac{1}{2}$ pint* in letters $\frac{1}{4}$" high

D. jar filled with hard candy with a label stating *contents—1 lb. avoir.* in letters $\frac{1}{2}$" high

Question 17.

DIRECTIONS: Question 17 is to be answered SOLELY on the basis of the information contained in the following passage.

DEALERS IN SECOND HAND DEVICES

1. It shall be unlawful for any person to engage in or conduct the business of dealing in, trading in, selling, receiving, or repairing condemned, rebuilt, or used weighing or measuring devices without a permit therefor.

2. Such permit shall expire on the twenty-eighth day of February next succeeding the date of issuance thereof.

3. Every person engaged in the above business, within five days after the making of a repair, or the sale and delivery of a repaired, rebuilt, or used weighing or measuring device, shall serve notice in writing on the commissioner giving the name and address of the person for whom the repair has been made or to whom a repaired, rebuilt, or used weighing or measuring device has been sold or delivered, and shall include a statement that such device has been so altered, repaired, or rebuilt as to conform to the regulations of the department.

17. According to the above passage, the MOST accurate of the following statements is: 17.____

    A. A permit issued to engage in the business mentioned above, first issued on April 23, 1968, expired on February 28, 1969.
    B. A rebuilt or repaired weighing or measuring device should not operate with less error than the tolerances permitted by the regulations of the department.
    C. If a used scale in good condition is sold, it is not necessary for the seller to notify the commissioner of the name and address of the buyer.
    D. There is a difference in the time required to notify the commissioner of a repair or of a sale of a repaired device.

Questions 18-19.

DIRECTIONS: Questions 18 and 19 are to be answered SOLELY on the basis of the following passage.

   A. It shall be unlawful for any person, firm, or corporation to sell or offer for sale at retail for use in internal combustion engines in motor vehicles any gasoline unless such seller shall post and keep continuously posted on the individual pump or other dispensing device from which such gasoline is sold or offered for sale a sign or placard not less than seven inches in height and eight inches in width nor larger than twelve inches in height and twelve inches in width and stating clearly in numbers of uniform size the selling price or prices per gallon of such gasoline so sold or offered for sale from such pump or other dispensing device.

B. The amount of governmental tax to be collected in connection with the sale of such gasoline shall be stated on such sign or placard and separately and apart from such selling price or prices.

18. The one of the following price signs posted on a gasoline pump which would be in violation of the above passage is a sign _____ square inches in size and _____ inches high.

   A. 144; 12   B. 84; 7   C. 72; 12   D. 60; 8

19. According to the above passage, the LEAST accurate of the following statements is:

   A. Gasoline may be sold from a dispensing device other than a pump.
   B. If two different pumps are used to sell the same grade of gasoline, a price sign must appear on each pump.
   C. The amount of governmental tax and the price of the gasoline must not be stated on the same sign.
   D. The sizes of the numbers used on a sign to indicate the price of gasoline must be the same.

Questions 20-21.

DIRECTIONS: Questions 20 and 21 are to be answered SOLELY on the basis of the following passage.

In all systems of weights and measures based on one or more arbitrary fundamental units, the concrete representation of the unit in the form of a standard is necessary, and the construction and preservation of such a standard is a matter of primary importance. Therefore, it is essential that the standard should be so constructed as to be as nearly permanent and invariable as human ingenuity can contrive. The reference of all measures to an original standard is essential for their correctness, and such a standard must be maintained and preserved in its integrity by some responsible authority which is thus able to provide against the use of false weights and measures. Accordingly, from earliest times, standards were constructed and preserved under the direction of kings and priests, and the temples were a favorite place for their deposit. Later, this duty was assumed by the government, and today we find the integrity of standards of weights and measures safeguarded by international agreement.

20. Of the following, the MOST valid implication which can be made on the basis of the above passage is that

   A. fundamental units of systems of weights and measures should be represented by quantities so constructed that they are specific and constant
   B. in the earliest times, standards were so constructed that they were as permanent and invariable as modern ones
   C. international agreement has practically relieved the U.S. government of the necessity of preserving standards of weights and measures
   D. the preservation of standards is of less importance than the ingenuity used in their construction

21. Of the following, the MOST appropriate title for the above passage is 21.____

    A. THE CONSTRUCTION AND PRESERVATION OF STANDARDS OF WEIGHTS AND MEASURES
    B. THE FIXING OF RESPONSIBILITY FOR THE ESTABLISHMENT OF STANDARDS OF WEIGHTS AND MEASURES
    C. THE HISTORY OF SYSTEMS OF WEIGHTS AND MEASURES
    D. THE VALUE OF PROPER STANDARDS IN PROVIDING CORRECT WEIGHTS AND MEASURES

Questions 22-23.

DIRECTIONS: Questions 22 and 23 are to be answered SOLELY on the basis of the following passage.

Accurate weighing and good scales insure that excess is not given just for the sake of good measure. No more striking example of the fundamental importance of correct weighing to the business man is found than in the simple and usual relation where a charge or value is obtained by multiplying a weight by a unit price. For example, a scale may weigh *light,* that is, the actual quantity delivered is in excess by 1 percent. The actual result is that the seller taxes himself. If his profit is supposed to be 10 percent of total sales, an overweight of 1 percent represents 10 percent of that profit. Under these conditions, the situation is as though the seller were required to pay a sales tax equivalent to what he is taxing himself.

22. Of the following, the MOST valid implication which can be made on the basis of the above passage is that 22.____

    A. consistent use of scales that weigh *light* will reduce sellers' profits
    B. no good businessman would give any buyer more than the weight required even if his scale is accurate
    C. the kind of situation described in the above passage could not arise if sales were being made of merchandise sold by the yard
    D. the use of incorrect scales is one of the reasons causing governments to impose sales taxes

23. According to the above passage, the MOST accurate of the following statements is: 23.____

    A. If his scale weighs *light* by an amount of 2 percent, the seller would deliver only 98 pounds when 100 pounds was the amount agreed upon.
    B. If the seller's scale weighs *heavy,* the buyer will receive an amount in excess of what he intended to purchase.
    C. If the seller's scale weighs *light* by an amount of 1 percent, a buyer who agreed to purchase 50 pounds of merchandise would actually receive $50 \frac{1}{2}$ pounds.
    D. The use of a scale which delivers an amount which is in excess of that required is an example of deliberate fraud.

Questions 24-25.

DIRECTIONS: Questions 24 and 25 are to be answered SOLELY on the basis of the following passage.

Food shall be deemed to be misbranded:
1. If its labeling is false or misleading in any particular.

2. If any word, statement, or other information required by or under authority of this article to appear on the label or labeling is not prominently placed thereon with such conspicuousness (as compared with other words, statements, designs, or devices in the labeling) and in such terms as to render it likely to be read and understood by the ordinary individual under customary conditions of purchase and use.

3. If it purports to be or is represented as a food for which a standard of quality has been prescribed and its quality falls below such standard, unless its label bears a statement that it falls below such standard.

24. According to the above passage, the MOST accurate of the following statements is:

    A. A food may be considered misbranded if the label contains a considerable amount of information which is not required.
    B. If a consumer purchased one type of canned food, although he intended to buy another, the food is probably misbranded.
    C. If a food is used in large amounts by a group of people of certain foreign origin, it can be considered misbranded unless the label is in the foreign language with which they are familiar.
    D. The required information on a label is likely to be in larger print than other information which may appear on it.

25. According to the above passage, the one of the following foods which may be considered to be misbranded is a

    A. can of peaches with a label which carries the brand name of the packer but states *Below Standard in Quality*
    B. can of vegetables with a label on which is printed a shield which states *U.S. Grade B*
    C. package of frozen food which has some pertinent information printed on it in very small type which a customer cannot read and which the store manager cannot read when asked to do so by the customer
    D. package of margarine of the same size as the usual package of butter, kept near the butter, but clearly labeled as margarine

KEY (CORRECT ANSWERS)

1. C
2. D
3. B
4. B
5. B

6. A
7. D
8. C
9. D
10. A

11. C
12. A
13. B
14. A
15. B

16. D
17. A
18. C
19. C
20. A

21. D
22. A
23. C
24. D
25. C

READING COMPREHENSION
UNDERSTANDING AND INTERPRETING WRITTEN MATERIAL
EXAMINATION SECTION
TEST 1

DIRECTIONS: Each question or incomplete statement is followed by several suggested answers or completions. Select the one that *BEST* answers the question or completes the statement. *PRINT THE LETTER OF THE CORRECT ANSWER IN THE SPACE AT THE RIGHT.*

Questions 1-5.

DIRECTIONS: The following passage is to be used as the *SOLE* basis for answering Questions 1 to 5. Read the selection carefully and base your answers *ONLY* on the information contained therein.

PASSAGE

Politicians, preachers, and moralists frequently inveigh against the breakdown of family and community morality. According to one variant of this position, it is because of a "moral breakdown" that we find so much "crime in the streets." This line of reasoning has a persuasive message for many white Americans – it carries surface plausibility and underlying racial prejudice. Family "breakdown," "immoral" delinquent gangs and African-Americans are all disproportionately found in the urban slums. There is, however, an important flaw in the implied argument of this modern morality tale. It is apparent that lower-class families have difficulty in maintaining control over their children. According to the modern morality tale, if parents were more responsible and less perverse, and exercised control over their children, there would be less delinquency. The parents, and later their children, are the villains. But the lack of control stems not from parental perversity but from parental poverty, that is, from the deprivations of lower-class status. Of course, personalities do vary, even in their degree of "perversity"; and there are undoubtedly elements of "perversity" among some parents who do not maintain control over their children. But the magnitude of the problem stems from major social forces that have a pervasive influence over the lives of so many people.

By increasing the amount and awareness of legitimate opportunities, and reducing the attractiveness of delinquent gangs and illegitimate behavior, it may be possible to reduce delinquency. But overcoming these deprivations may also have an indirect effect upon delinquency by influencing family structure. The key problem in the lower class family is the weak occupational economic position of the man. Since, in the United States, the man is expected to be the breadwinner above all else, he performs inadequately at his major role within the family. As a result the lower class man is not esteemed, even within his own family. Under these circumstances, he may also leave his family. It can therefore be expected that improvements made in occupational and economic opportunities for lower class men will strengthen their position within the family and thereby strengthen the stability of the family as a whole. It will also heighten the attractiveness of the father and the family in the eyes of the children and make additional resources available within the family. Such changes will make it possible for the family to maintain stronger controls over its children.

Some argue that the provision of opportunities is not enough–that lower class people differ in their subculture, or values, or goals, or motivations so that they would not take advantage of these opportunities. Although value modifications generally take place within the lower class to make life's values more in accord with life's circumstances, it appears that middle class values and goals are still retained. Lower class people frequently find it necessary to stretch their values and aspirations downward to accord with realistic opportunities, but they do not abandon middle class values. They may lessen their commitment to values so that some of the sting will be taken out of life's deprivations, but they do not abandon all values. In short, providing additional opportunities seems to be the key area for change.

QUESTIONS

1. According to the passage, which of the following statements concerning street crime and moral breakdown is CORRECT?

    A. The irresponsibility of parents in slum-areas is the root cause of moral breakdown and street crime.
    B. Moral breakdown is basically a result of street crime.
    C. Moral breakdown and street crime are aspects of larger and widespread social problems.
    D. Street crime is basically a result of moral breakdown.
    E. Moral breakdown and street crime are a response to the prejudice of many white Americans.

2. According to the passage, the problem of juvenile delinquency is basically a result of

    A. the overrepresentation of minority groups in lower class neighborhoods
    B. the poor social and economic conditions that are an inherent part of lower class life
    C. the unwillingness of parents to accept their responsibilities and exercise discipline
    D. the breakdown in family morality that is most pervasive among the lower class
    E. personality variations among lower class parents which prevent them from maintaining control over their children

3. According to the passage, the *central* problem of the lower class family is the

    A. absence of goal motivated behavior
    B. failure to develop a distinct subculture within poor communities
    C. dissatisfaction with middle class values
    D. inability of the father to adequately support his family
    E. attractiveness of delinquency and illegitimate behavior

4. According to the passage, providing greater occupational opportunities for lower class men will result in all of the following EXCEPT

    A. allowing families to maintain greater control over their children
    B. improving the standing of lower class fathers within their families
    C. reducing the amount of juvenile delinquency so that lower class neighborhoods are as safe as others in the city
    D. increasing the stability of lower class families
    E. enhancing the image of the family itself for lower class children

5. According to the passage, lower class people often make adjustments in their values. As a result, their values *generally* 5._____

   A. reflect the opportunities that are actually available to the lower class
   B. coincide exactly with middle class values
   C. depend upon a family structure that lacks a strong father figure
   D. include goals and aspirations that exceed their economic situation
   E. deny responsibility for the delinquent behavior of their children

Questions 6-10.

DIRECTIONS: Questions 6 to 10 are to be answered *SOLELY* on the basis of the following passage.

PASSAGE

Of all the groups claiming interference by restrictions on the dissemination of news, the one with the most pressing claim is the law enforcement agency. Due to the combination of a morbid interest in crimes of violence and fear that a vicious criminal may be at large, there is a demand by the public for a showing by the police of capability in solving a crime. Perhaps unwilling to acknowledge the existence of, and accept responsibility for, a degenerate element in its midst, the public tends to cast the blame for a successful crime on police failure to prevent it. Thus there is constant pressure on the police to demonstrate that the case is nearing solution and that the perpetrator will soon be in custody. To avoid the accusation of suppressing information to cover up malfeasance, there is a legitimate tendency on the part of the police to cooperate with the press and thus escape being cast in an unfavorable light. The ideal solution – from the point of view of the police – would be to allow them free rein in releasing information to reassure the public. However, this would not be consonant with the right of the accused to a fair trial with the presumption of innocence.

A distinguished committee of lawyers and jurists has developed a comprehensive code for police and law enforcement agencies. The committee's recommendations include the following:

A. Concerning the Defendant
   1. The release of information concerning the defendant shall be limited to his name, age, occupation, marital status, and personal data not related to the crime or the character of the defendant. His criminal record, prior medical and psychiatric history, or military disciplinary record, if any, shall not be released. No other information that is clearly prejudicial to the defendant shall be released.
   2. No statement of any nature made by the defendant, or the substance thereof, shall be released. No reference shall be made to any test taken by the defendant or that he has refused to take.
   3. The announcement of the arrest of the defendant may include, in addition to the information authorized above, the time, place, and manner of apprehension as well as the text or summary of the charge, information, or indictment. No comments shall be made relating to his guilt or innocence.
   4. News media shall not be permitted to interview the defendant with or without his attorney's consent, while he is in police custody.
   5. News media shall not be permitted to photograph or televise the defendant while he is in police custody except in a public place. This prohibition extends to such instances as where he is being interrogated, where he is being processed ("booked") following arrest, where he is in a lockup or detention facility, or where he is at a hospital bedside for identification purposes.
   6. Where the defendant is still at large, and it appears that he is a fugitive from justice, additional information that may reasonably and directly aid in effecting his apprehension, including his photograph, may be released.

B. Concerning the Crime, the Investigation, and the Arrest
1. A general description of the crime shall be made available to the news media. Gruesome or sordid aspects which tend unduly to inflame public emotions shall not be released. Witnesses shall not be identified by name or otherwise, nor shall any comment be made concerning their credibility, their testimony, or their identification of the defendant.
2. No comment on the apparent motivation or character of the perpetrator shall be made.
3. No information concerning scientific evidence such as laboratory or ballistics tests or fingerprints shall be released.

C. General
1. A member of the police agency shall be designated as the Information Officer responsible for the dissemination of all information to the news media. It will be the responsibility of the Information Officer to supervise the enforcement of these regulations and to solicit and encourage full cooperation of news media. No member of a police agency may furnish any information to news media without prior approval by the Information Officer. No interviews shall be permitted with investigating or arresting officers.
2. Wherever feasible, the Information Officer will encourage news media to enter into pool arrangements so as to reduce confusion and interference with the orderly processes of law enforcement. It shall be a prime responsibility of the Information Officer to insure a calm and orderly atmosphere during the dissemination of information to the news media.

QUESTIONS

6. According to the passage, the tendency of the police to cooperate with the press by releasing information is based on the

   A. public's desire for evidence that the police are able to bring criminals to justice
   B. deterrent effect on other criminals which results from reports of police efficiency
   C. requirement of the courts for full disclosure of pertinent information
   D. assistance which unrestricted publicity provides in apprehending perpetrators who are still at large
   E. belief that charges of corruption cannot be avoided in any other way

7. Of the following, the *BASIC* purpose of the recommendations contained in the passage is to

   A. satisfy the public's curiosity concerning crime
   B. expedite the dissemination of information to the news media
   C. protect the defendant's right to a fair trial
   D. enhance the reputation of the police
   E. reduce interference by the news media in essential police functions

8. According to the recommendations contained in the passage, it would *NOT* be proper for a law enforcement agency to

   A. release information pertaining to how the defendant was caught
   B. discuss the testimony given by eyewitnesses
   C. distribute a written copy or synopsis of the indictment
   D. provide a general description of the crime in question
   E. disclose the occupation and marital status of the defendant

9. According to the recommendations contained in the passage, law enforcement agencies, under certain circumstances, would be able to

   A. permit a defendant to make a statement to the news media
   B. release information concerning the defendant's medical history which is not pertinent to the case
   C. describe to the news media evidence against the defendant in terms of probable guilt or innocence
   D. allow a defendant to be televised while in their custody in a non-public place
   E. provide a photograph of the defendant to the news media

10. According to the passage, the Information Officer in a police department is responsible for all of the following EXCEPT

    A. coordinating interviews of arresting officers by members of the news media
    B. enforcing regulations concerning dissemination of information to the news media
    C. fostering the use of pool arrangements by the news media
    D. approving in advance all requests by the news media for information
    E. preventing hectic and unruly situations when information is provided to the news media.

KEY (CORRECT ANSWERS)

1.	C	6.	A
2.	B	7.	C
3.	D	8.	B
4.	C	9.	E
5.	A	10.	A

TEST 2

DIRECTIONS: Each question or incomplete statement is followed by several suggested answers or completions. Select the one that *BEST* answers the question or completes the statement. *PRINT THE LETTER OF THE CORRECT ANSWER IN THE SPACE AT THE RIGHT.*

Questions 1-5.

DIRECTIONS: Questions 1 to 5 are to be answered *SOLELY* on the basis of the following passage.

PASSAGE

There is a hazy boundary between grateful citizens paying their respects to a proud profession, and "good" citizens involved in corruption, wishing to buy future favors. Once begun, however, the acceptance of small bribes and favors or similar practices can become "norms" or informal standards of cliques of policemen. A recruit can be socialized into accepting these illegal practices by mild, informal negative sanctions such as the withholding of group acceptance. If these unlawful practices are embraced, the recruit's membership group – the police force – and his reference group – the clique involved in illegal behavior – are no longer one and the same. In such circumstances the norms of the reference group (the illegal-oriented clique) would clearly take precedence over either the formal requisites of the membership group (police department regulations) or the formalized norms (legal statutes) of the larger society. When such conflicts are apparent a person can

1. conform to one, take the consequences of non-conformity to the other;
2. seek a compromise position by which he attempts to conform in part, though not wholly, to one or more sets of role expectations, in the hope that sanctions applied will be minimal.

If these reference group norms involving illegal activity become routinized with use they become an identifiable informal "code." Such codes are not unique to the police profession. A fully documented case study of training at a military academy, in which an informal pattern of behavior was assimilated along with the formal standards, clearly outlined the function of the informal norms, their dominance when in conflict with formal regulations, and the secretive nature of their existence to facilitate their effectiveness and subsequent preservation. This same secrecy could be demanded of a police "code" to insure its preservation. Although within the clique the code must be well defined, the ignorance of the lay public to even its existence would be a requisite to its continuous and effective use. Through participation in activity regimented by the "code," an increased group identity and cohesion among "code" practitioners would emerge.

Group identity requires winning of acceptance as a member of the inner group and, thereby, gaining access to the secrets of the occupation which are acquired through informal contacts with colleagues. Lack of this acceptance not only bars the neophyte from the inner secrets of the profession, but may isolate him socially and professionally from his colleagues and even his superiors. There is the added fear that, in some circumstances in which he would need their support, they would avoid becoming involved, forcing him to face personal danger or public ridicule alone.

QUESTIONS

1. According to the passage, the reference group of a recruit who accepts corrupt practices is

   A. the police force of which the recruit is a member
   B. a loosely-structured group from which the recruit learns both formal and informal norms
   C. the coterie of officers who are involved in illegal activities
   D. society as a whole, of which the police are a component
   E. a professional organization which instructs the recruit in his responsibilities

   1.____

2. According to the passage, allegiance by policemen to informally codified standards of behavior is *most likely* to result in

   A. increased attempts by most citizens to bribe police officers
   B. a decrease of mutual support among policemen
   C. greater awareness on the part of the public of such behavior
   D. decreased secrecy about police department practices
   E. stronger group identification among such policemen

   2.____

3. According to the passage, the police recuit who is NOT accepted by the group which is involved in illegal behavior will

   A. be prevented from learning many confidential aspects of police work
   B. face less risk of public ridicule or personal danger
   C. be held in high esteem by his superiors
   D. gain social and professional stature among his colleagues
   E. be more likely to expose the activities of the group to the public

   3.____

4. According to the passage, informal codes of illegal behavior function effectively only when they

   A. are tacitly accepted by the entire society
   B. permit formal standards to predominate whenever there is a conflict
   C. exist without being known to outsiders
   D. minimize the use of informal negative sanctions
   E. complement pre-existing norms within the police profession

   4.____

5. According to the passage, a recruit who must deal with conflicting norms of different groups may

   A. not be able to distinguish between ordinary citizens and those involved in graft
   B. try to accommodate himself to the different roles he is expected to play
   C. be unaware of the informal codes of behavior within the police department
   D. accept one set of standards and thereby avoid any unpleasant consequences
   E. find that he is able to solve the problem by bringing the competing norms into conformity

   5.____

Questions 6-10.

DIRECTIONS: Questions 6 to 10 are to be answered *SOLELY* on the basis of the following passage.

PASSAGE

THE CONCEPT OF AN OFFENSIVELY DEPLOYED PATROL FORCE

Police forces, in general, are defensively deployed, both in their organization and operation. That is, they are principally designed to act efficiently during or after the commission of a crime. This concept becomes quite clear when the distribution of available manpower of a police force is examined.

The defensive enforcement attitude is prevalent in the philosophy of the individual policeman. Most law enforcement officers seem to view the making of an arrest as one of their major goals. The reason for this attitude is obvious. Police administrators do not have available a measuring technique for evaluating an officer's crime prevention efforts, while an arrest is a measure of his defensive effectiveness.

One of the most serious drawbacks for any police force that is committed to a defensive action during a period of rising crime, is that it becomes, of necessity, a retrograde operation; that is, as more crime is committed, more manpower is utilized for investigation, with a corresponding decrease in crime prevention activities, thus encouraging more crime, more manpower for investigation, etc., etc. The logical extension of this situation is a police force that is completely overloaded with investigations, while crime runs rampant.

It is now appropriate to inquire into the effectiveness of defensive police strategy in the present crime situation. Determining the effectiveness of a police system and its strategy requires the use of absolute measurements. In particular, the effectiveness should be measured in terms of how well it attains its goals. By these measures, the defensive strategy used by the police does not appear to be effective.

If the goal of police action is to eliminate or substantially reduce crime, it is not succeeding. The number of crimes as well as the crime rate is increasing.

It seems completely self-evident that if it were possible to station a policeman at or about every house and building in the city, the amount of crime would be significantly reduced. It would be reduced not because a criminal would be caught after he committed a crime, but because he would not commit the crime, because of the fear of being caught. Thus the crime rate would be reduced by preventing the crime from happening, not by punishing the criminal (if caught) after the crime has been committed.

The solution is, of course, not a practical one but, nevertheless, it should serve as an ideal for an offensively deployed police force. In practice, the force should create the appearance of being everywhere at once.

In contrast to the defensive force, whose operation is retrograde, such an offensive force would be progressive in nature; that is, by preventing a crime from occurring, the manpower required for investigation would be reduced. Hence, it could be diverted toward the prevention of more crime, which would further reduce the investigations and manpower needed, etc. The logical extension of this situation is a force that is completely deployed to prevent crime.

The offensive force depicted above is, of course, a patrol force, but not in the sense of the conventional police patrol, which is very inflexible with regard to the time and place it can be deployed, which is heavily committed to answering complaints, and which is managed by "seat of the pants" techniques.

The specifications for an offensively deployed patrol force are as follows:
1. A patrol unit must pass by every point in the city, on the average of once every ten minutes.

2. The patrol unit must not be sent on a complaint, unless the complaint can be disposed of in less than ten minutes, or there is a crime or equivalent emergency situation in progress. If a unit does become involved, its territory must be covered by adjacent patrol units.
3. The patrol force must be deployed with due regard to the expected type and location of crime, based on an analysis of previous criminal activity for the particular season of the year, day of the week, hour of the day, etc.

QUESTIONS

6. Assume that a certain city has changed the nature of its motor patrol force from a defensive force to offensive deployment.
Which one of the following results will MOST logically follow if the patrol force is functioning in line with the principles discussed in the passage? The

   A. arrest rate for burglary will decrease
   B. number of complaints received will increase
   C. number of aggravated assaults will increase
   D. number of miles that the patrol vehicles travel will increase
   E. number of complaints answered by the patrol force will increase

7. According to the passage, which one of the following MOST accurately states the underlying purpose of offensively deployed patrol? To

   A. leave the patrol unit free to perform offensive patrol
   B. increase the number of criminals that are caught and punished
   C. catch so many criminals that the criminals are afraid to commit offenses
   D. make offenders so fearful of being caught that they refrain from committing offenses
   E. have a patrol unit pass every point in the city on the average of once every ten minutes

8. A certain police department has accepted the concept of offensive deployment. In implementing this concept, it has adopted a policy defining the basic responsibility for making initial investigations or crimes.
Which one of the following is MOST likely the policy this department has adopted, if it followed the terms of the passage?

   A. Basic responsibility for initial investigation of crimes is assigned to the patrol force.
   B. Basic responsibility for initial criminal investigation is assigned somewhere other than to the patrol units.
   C. As crime increases above normal levels, the basic responsibility for initial investigation of crime retrogrades to the patrol force.
   D. As crime increases above normal levels, the basic responsibility for initial investigation of crime retrogrades to the Detective Division.
   E. When crime is normal, basic responsibility for initial investigation of crime is divided between the Detective Division and the patrol force, depending on the availability of manpower in each.

9. Assume the following facts: The police department of a certain city has implemented the concept of an offensively deployed police force based on the recommendations contained in the passage.
Which one of the following results would MOST logically indicate that the patrol force is functioning ineffectively? The

   A. crime rate has decreased
   B. number of crime investigations by the patrol units has increased
   C. percentage of crimes cleared by arrest has increased
   D. number of prosecutions for crimes cleared by arrest has increased
   E. average amount of time spent by the average officer answering complaints has decreased

10. According to the passage, which one of the following is the MOST probable reason why many individual policemen have accepted the philosophy of defensive enforcement? Because

    A. of the retrograde philosophy
    B. no technique exists for evaluating an officer's offensive efforts
    C. most policemen believe in the effectiveness of the crime-investigation cycle
    D. the goal of police action is to eliminate or substantially reduce crime
    E. the effectiveness of defensive police strategy has never been evaluated

KEY (CORRECT ANSWERS)

1. C
2. E
3. A
4. C
5. B

6. D
7. D
8. B
9. B
10. B

PREPARING WRITTEN MATERIAL

PARAGRAPH REARRANGEMENT
COMMENTARY

The sentences that follow are in scrambled order. You are to rearrange them in proper order and indicate the letter choice containing the correct answer at the space at the right.

Each group of sentences in this section is actually a paragraph presented in scrambled order. Each sentence in the group has a place in that paragraph; no sentence is to be left out. You are to read each group of sentences and decide upon the best order in which to put the sentences so as to form a well-organized paragraph.

The questions in this section measure the ability to solve a problem when all the facts relevant to its solution are not given.

More specifically, certain positions of responsibility and authority require the employee to discover connection between events sometimes, apparently, unrelated. In order to do this, the employee will find it necessary to correctly infer that unspecified events have probably occurred or are likely to occur. This ability becomes especially important when action must be taken on incomplete information.

Accordingly, these questions require competitors to choose among several suggested alternatives, each of which presents a different sequential arrangement of the events. Competitors must choose the MOST logical of the suggested sequences.

In order to do so, they may be required to draw on general knowledge to infer missing concepts or events that are essential to sequencing the given events. Competitors should be careful to infer only what is essential to the sequence. The plausibility of the wrong alternatives will always require the inclusion of unlikely events or of additional chains of events which are NOT essential to sequencing the given events.

It's very important to remember that you are looking for the best of the four possible choices, and that the best choice of all may not even be one of the answers you're given to choose from.

There is no one right way to solve these problems. Many people have found it helpful to first write out the order of the sentences, as they would have arranged them, on their scrap paper before looking at the possible answers. If their optimum answer is there, this can save them some time. If it isn't, this method can still give insight into solving the problem. Others find it most helpful to just go through each of the possible choices, contrasting each as they go along. You should use whatever method feels comfortable and works for you.

While most of these types of questions are not that difficult, we've added a higher percentage of the difficult type, just to give you more practice. Usually there are only one or two questions on this section that contain such subtle distinctions that you're unable to answer confidently. And you then may find yourself stuck deciding between two possible choices, neither of which you're sure about.

EXAMINATION SECTION

TEST 1

DIRECTIONS: Each question consists of several sentences which can be arranged in a logical sequence. For each question, select the choice which places the numbered sentences in the MOST logical sequence. *PRINT THE LETTER OF THE CORRECT ANSWER IN THE SPACE AT THE RIGHT.*

1. I. A body was found in the woods.
   II. A man proclaimed innocence.
   III. The owner of a gun was located.
   IV. A gun was traced.
   V. The owner of a gun was questioned.
   The CORRECT answer is:
   A. IV, III, V, II, I
   B. II, I, IV, III, V
   C. I, IV, III, V, II
   D. I, III, V, II, IV
   E. I, II, IV, III, V

   1.____

2. I. A man is in a hunting accident.
   II. A man fell down a flight of steps.
   III. A man lost his vision in one eye,
   IV. A man broke his leg.
   V. A man had to walk with a cane.
   The CORRECT answer is:
   A. II, IV, V, I, III
   B. IV, V, I, III, II
   C. III, I, IV, V, II
   D. I, III, V, II, IV
   E. I, III, II, IV, V

   2.____

3. I. A man is offered a new job.
   II. A woman is offered a new job.
   III. A man works as a waiter.
   IV. A woman works as a waitress.
   V. A woman gives notice.
   The CORRECT answer is:
   A. IV, II, V, III, I
   B. IV, II, V, I, III
   C. II, IV, V, III, I
   D. III, I, IV, II, V
   E. IV, III, II, V, I

   3.____

4. I. A train let the station late.
   II. A man was late for work.
   III. A man lost his job.
   IV. Many people complained because the train was late.
   V. There was a traffic jam.
   The CORRECT answer is:
   A. V, II, I, IV, III
   B. V, I, IV, II, III
   C. V, I, II, IV, III
   D. I, V, IV, II, III
   E. II, I, IV, V, III

   4.____

5. I. The burden of proof as to each issue is determined before trial and remains upon the same party throughout the trial.
    II. The jury is at liberty to believe one witness' testimony as against a number of contradictory witnesses.
    III. In a civil case, the party bearing the burden of proof is required to prove his contention by a fair preponderance of the evidence.
    IV. However, it must be noted that a fair preponderance of evidence does not necessarily mean a greater number of witnesses.
    V. The burden of proof is the burden which rests upon one of the parties to an action to persuade the trier of the facts, generally the jury, that a proposition he asserts is true.
    VI. If the evidence is equally balanced, or if it leaves the jury in such doubt as to be unable to decide the controversy either way, judgment must be given against the party upon whom the burden of proof rests.
    The CORRECT answer is:
       A. III. II, V, IV, I, VI   B. I, II, VI, V, III, IV   C. III, IV, V, I, II, VI
       D. V, I, III, VI, IV, II   E. I, V, III, VI, IV, II

6. I. If a parent is without assets and is unemployed, he cannot be convicted of the crime of non-support of a child.
    II. The term *sufficient ability* has been held to mean sufficient financial ability.
    III. It does not matter if his unemployment is by choice or unavoidable circumstances.
    IV. If he fails to take any steps at all, he may be liable to prosecution for endangering the welfare of a child.
    V. Under the penal law, a parent is responsible for the support of his minor child only if the parent is of *sufficient ability*.
    VI. An indigent parent may meet his obligation by borrowing money or by seeking aid under the provisions of the Social Welfare Law.
    The CORRECT answer is:
       A. VI, I, V, III, II, IV   B. I, III, V, II, IV, VI   C. V, II, I, III, VI, IV
       D. I, VI, IV, V, II, III   E. II, V, I, III, VI, IV

7. I. Consider, for example, the case of a rabble rouser who urges a group of twenty people to go out and break the windows of a nearby factory.
    II. Therefore, the law fills the indicated gap with the crime of *inciting to riot*.
    III. A person is considered guilty of inciting to riot when he urges ten or more persons to engage in tumultuous and violent conduct of a kind likely to create public alarm.
    IV. However, if he has not obtained the cooperation of at least four people, he cannot be charged with unlawful assembly.
    V. The charge of inciting to riot was added to the law to cover types of conduct which cannot be classified as either the crime of *riot* or the crime of *unlawful assembly*.
    VI. If he acquires the acquiescence of at least four of them, he is guilty of unlawful assembly even if the project does not materialize.
    The CORRECT answer is:
       A. III, V, I, VI, IV, II   B. V, I, IV, VI, II, III   C. III, IV, I, V, II, VI
       D. V, I, IV, VI, III, II   E. V, III, I, VI, IV, II

8. I. If, however, the rebuttal evidence presents an issue of credibility, it is for the jury to determine whether the presumption has, in fact, been destroyed.
    II. Once sufficient evidence to the contrary is introduced, the presumption disappears from the trial.
    III. The effect of a presumption is to place the burden upon the adversary to come forward with evidence to rebut the presumption.
    IV. When a presumption is overcome and ceases to exist in the case, the fact or facts which gave rise to the presumption still remain.
    V. Whether a presumption has been overcome is ordinarily a question for the court.
    VI. Such information may furnish a basis for a logical inference.
    The CORRECT answer is:
       A. IV, VI, II, V, I, III   B. III, II, V, I, IV, VI   C. V, III, VI, IV, II, I
       D. V, IV, I, II, VI, III   E. II, III, V, I, IV, VI

8.____

9. I. An executive may answer a letter by writing his reply on the face of the letter itself instead of having a return letter typed.
    II. This procedure is efficient because it saves the executive's time, the typist's time, and saves office file space.
    III. Copying machines are used in small offices as well as large offices to save time and money in making brief replies to business letters.
    IV. A copy is made on a copying machine to go into the company files, while the original is mailed back to the sender.
    The CORRECT answer is:
       A. I, II, IV, III   B. I, IV, II, III   C. III, I, IV, II   D. III, IV, II, I

9.____

10. I. Most organizations favor one of the types but always include the others to a lesser degree.
    II. However, we can detect a definite trend toward greater use of symbolic control.
    III. We suggest that our local police agencies are today primarily utilizing material control.
    IV. Control can be classified into three types: physical, material, and symbolic.
    The CORRECT answer is:
       A. IV, II, III, I   B. II, I, IV, III   C. III, IV, II, I   D. IV, I, III, II

10.____

11. I. Project residents had first claim to this use, followed by surrounding neighborhood children.
    II. By contrast, recreation space within the project's interior was found to be used more often by both groups.
    III. Studies of the use of project grounds in many cities showed grounds left open for public use were neglected and unused, both by residents and by members of the surrounding community.
    IV. Project residents had clearly laid claim to the play spaces, setting up and enforcing unwritten rules for use.
    V. Each group, by experience, found their activities easily disrupted by other groups, and their claim to the use of space for recreation difficult to enforce.

11.____

The CORRECT answer is:
A. IV, V, I, II, III   B. V, II, IV, III, I
C. I, IV, III, II, V   D. III, V, II, IV, I

12. I. They do not consider the problems correctable within the existing subsidy formula and social policy of accepting all eligible applicants regardless of social behavior.
  II. A recent survey, however, indicated that tenants believe these problems correctable by local housing authorities and management within the existing financial formula.
  III. Many of the problems and complaints concerning public housing management and design have created resentment between the tenant and the landlord.
  IV. This same survey indicated that administrators and managers do not agree with the tenants.
  The CORRECT answer is:
  A. II, I, III, IV   B. I, III, IV, II   C. III, II, IV, I   D. IV, II, I, III

13. I. In single-family residences, there is usually enough distance between tenants to prevent occupants from annoying one another.
  II. For example, a certain small percentage of tenant families has one or more members addicted to alcohol.
  III. While managers believe in the right of individuals to live as they choose, the manager becomes concerned when the pattern of living jeopardizes others' rights.
  IV. Still others turn night into day, staging lusty entertainments which carry on into the hours when most tenants are trying to sleep.
  V. In apartment buildings, however, tenants live so closely together that any misbehavior can result in unpleasant living conditions.
  VI. Other families engage in violent argument.
  The CORRECT answer is:
  A. III, II, V, IV, VI, I   B. I, V, II, VI, IV, III
  C. II, V, IV, I, III, VI   D. IV, II, V, VI, III, I

14. I. Congress made the commitment explicit in the Housing Act of 194, establishing as a national goal the realization of a *decent home and suitable environment for every American family*.
  II. The result has been that the goal of decent home and suitable environment is still as far distant as ever for the disadvantaged urban family.
  III. In spite of this action by Congress, federal housing programs have continued to be fragmented and grossly underfunded.
  IV. The passage of the National Housing Act signaled a few federal commitment to provide housing for the nation's citizens.
  The CORRECT answer is:
  A. I, IV, III, II   B. IV, I, III, II   C. IV, I, II, III   D. II, IV, I, III

15.
I. The greater expense does not necessarily involve *exploitation*, but it is often perceived as exploitative and unfair by those who are aware of the price differences involved, but unaware of operating costs.
II. Ghetto residents believe they are *exploited* by local merchants, and evidence substantiates some of these beliefs.
III. However, stores in low-income areas were more likely to be small independents, which could not achieve the economies available to supermarket chains and were, therefore, more likely to charge higher prices, and the customers were more likely to buy smaller-sized packages which are more expensive per unit of measure.
IV. A study conducted in one city showed that distinctly higher prices were charged for goods sold in ghetto stores in other areas.

The CORRECT answer is:
  A. IV, II, I, III   B. IV, I, III, II   C. II, IV, III, I   D. II, III, IV, I

15.____

KEY (CORRECT ANSWERS)

1.	C	6.	C	11.	D
2.	E	7.	A	12.	C
3.	B	8.	B	13.	B
4.	B	9.	C	14.	B
5.	D	10.	D	15.	C

PREPARING WRITTEN MATERIAL
EXAMINATION SECTION
TEST 1

DIRECTIONS: Each question or incomplete statement is followed by several suggested answers or completions. Select the one that BEST answers the question or completes the statement. *PRINT THE LETTER OF THE CORRECT ANSWER IN THE SPACE AT THE RIGHT.*

Questions 1-4.

DIRECTIONS: Questions 1 through 4 each consist of a sentence which may or may not be an example of good English. The underlined parts of each sentence may be correct or incorrect. Examine each sentence, considering grammar, punctuation, spelling, and capitalization. If the English usage in the underlined parts of the sentence given is better than any of the changes in the underlined words suggested in options B, C, or D, choose option A. If the changes in the underlined words suggested in options B, C, or D would make the sentence correct, choose the correct option. Do not choose an option that will change the meaning of the sentence.

1. This Fall, the office will be closed on Columbus Day, October 9th. 1.____
   A. Correct as is
   B. fall...Columbus Day; October
   C. Fall...columbus day, October
   D. fall...Columbus Day – October

2. There weren't no paper in the supply closet. 2.____
   A. Correct as is
   B. weren't any
   C. wasn't any
   D. wasn't no

3. The alphabet, or A to Z sequence are the basis of most filing systems. 3.____
   A. Correct as is
   B. alphabet, or A to Z sequence, is
   C. alphabet, or A to Z sequence, are
   D. alphabet, or A too Z sequence, is

4. The Office Aide checked the register and finding the date of the meeting. 4.____
   A. Correct as is
   B. regaster and finding
   C. register and found
   D. regaster and found

Questions 5-10.

DIRECTIONS: Questions 5 through 10 consist of sentences which contain examples of correct or incorrect English usage. Examine each sentence with reference to grammar, spelling, punctuation, and capitalization. Chooses one of the following options that would be BEST for correct English usage:

2 (#1)

A. The sentence is correct
B. There is one mistake
C. There are two mistakes
D. There are three mistakes

5. Mrs. Fitzgerald came to the 59th Precinct to retreive her property which were stolen earlier in the week.   5.____

6. The two officer's responded to the call, only to find that the perpatrator and the victim have left the scene.   6.____

7. Mr. Coleman called the 61st Precinct to report that, upon arriving at his store, he discovered that there was a large hole in the wall and that three boxes of radios were missing.   7.____

8. The Administrative Leiutenant of the 62nd Precinct held a meeting which was attended by all the civilians, assigned to the Precinct.   8.____

9. Three days after the robbery occurred the detective apprahended two suspects and recovered the stolen items.   9.____

10. The Community Affairs Officer of the 64th Precinct is the liaison between the Precinct and the community; he works closely with various community organizations, and elected officials,   10.____

Questions 11-18.

DIRECTIONS: Questions 11 through 18 are to be answered on the basis of the following paragraph, which contains some deliberate errors in spelling and/or grammar and/or punctuation. Each line of the paragraph is preceded by a number. There are 9 lines and 9 numbers.

Line No.	Paragraph Line
1	The protection of life and proporty are, one of
2	the oldest and most important functions of a city.
3	New York City has it's own full-time police Agency.
4	The police Department has the power an it shall
5	be there duty to preserve the Public piece,
6	prevent crime detect and arrest offenders, supress
7	riots, protect the rites of persons and property, etc.
8	The maintainance of sound relations with the community they
9	serve is an important function of law enforcement officers

11. How many errors are contained in line one?   11.____

12. How many errors are contained in line two?   12.____

13. How many errors are contained in line three?   13.____

14. How many errors are contained in line four? 14._____

15. How many errors are contained in line five? 15._____

16. How many errors are contained in line six? 16._____

17. How many errors are contained in line seven? 17._____

18. How many errors are contained in line eight? 18._____

19. In the sentence, *The candidate wants to file his application for preference before it is too late*, the word *before* is used as a(n) 19._____
    A. preposition
    B. subordinating conjunction
    C. pronoun
    D. adverb

20. The one of the following sentences which is grammatically PREFERABLE to the others is: 20._____
    A. Our engineers will go over your blueprints so that you may have no problems in construction.
    B. For a long time he had been arguing that we, not he, are to blame for the confusion.
    C. I worked on this automobile for two hours and still cannot find out what is wrong with it.
    D. Accustomed to all kinds of hardships, fatigue seldom bothers veteran policemen.

KEY (CORRECT ANSWERS)

1.	A	11.	C
2.	C	12.	D
3.	B	13.	C
4.	C	14.	B
5.	C	15.	C
6.	D	16.	B
7.	A	17.	A
8.	C	18.	A
9.	C	19.	B
10.	B	20.	A

TEST 2

DIRECTIONS: Each question or incomplete statement is followed by several suggested answers or completions. Select the one that BEST answers the question or completes the statement. *PRINT THE LETTER OF THE CORRECT ANSWER IN THE SPACE AT THE RIGHT.*

1. The plural of
   A. turkey is turkies
   B. cargo is cargoes
   C. bankruptcy is bankruptcys
   D. son-in-law is son-in-laws

   1.____

2. The abbreviation *viz.* means MOST NEARLY
   A. namely   B. for example   C. the following   D. see

   2.____

3. In the sentence, *A man in a light-grey suit waited thirty-five minutes in the ante-room for the all-important document,* the word IMPROPERLY hyphenated is
   A. light-grey   B. thirty-five   C. ante-room   D. all-important

   3.____

4. The MOST accurate of the following sentences is:
   A. The commissioner, as well as his deputy and various bureau heads, were present.
   B. A new organization of employers and employees have been formed.
   C. One or the other of these men have been selected.
   D. The number of pages in the book is enough to discourage a reader.

   4.____

5. The MOST accurate of the following sentences is:
   A. Between you and me, I think he is the better man.
   B. He was believed to be me.
   C. Is it us that you wish to see?
   D. The winners are him and her.

   5.____

Questions 6-13.

DIRECTIONS: The sentences numbered 6 through 13 deal with some phase of police activity. They may be classified most appropriately under one of the following four categories.

   A. Faulty because of incorrect grammar
   B. Faulty because of incorrect punctuation
   C. Faulty because of incorrect use of a word
   D. Correct

Examine each sentence carefully. Then, in the space at the right, print the capital letter preceding the option which is the BEST of the four suggested above. All incorrect sentences contain only one type of error. Consider a sentence correct if it contains none of the types of errors mentioned, even though there may be other correct ways of expressing the same thought.

2 (#2)

6. The Department Medal of Honor is awarded to a member of the Police Force who distinguishes himself inconspicuously in the line of police duty by the performance of an act of gallantry.

6._____

7. Members of the Detective Division are charged with the prevention of crime, the detection and arrest of criminals and the recovery of lost or stolen property,

7._____

8. Detectives are selected from the uniformed patrol forces after they have indicated by conduct, aptitude and performance that they are qualified for the more intricate duties of a detective.

8._____

9. The patrolman, pursuing his assailant, exchanged shots with the gunman and immortally wounded him as he fled into a nearby building.

9._____

10. The members of the Traffic Division has to enforce the Vehicle and Traffic Law, the Traffic Regulations and ordinances relating to vehicular and pedestrian traffic.

10._____

11. After firing a shot at the gunman, the crowd dispersed from the patrolman's line of fire.

11._____

12. The efficiency of the Missing Persons Bureau is maintained with a maximum of public personnel due to the specialized training given to its members.

12._____

13. Records of persons arrested for violations of Vehicle and Traffic Regulations are transmitted upon request to precincts, courts and other authorized agencies.

13._____

14. Following are two sentences which may or may not be written in correct English:
    I. Two clients assaulted the officer.
    II. The van is illegally parked.
  Which one of the following statements is CORRECT?
    A. Only Sentence I is written in correct English.
    B. Only Sentence II is written in correct English.
    C. Sentences I and II are both written in correct English.
    D. Neither Sentence I nor Sentence II is written in correct English.

14._____

15. Following are two sentences which may or may not be written in correct English:
    I. Security Officer Rollo escorted the visitor to the patrolroom.
    II. Two entry were made in the facility logbook.
  Which one of the following statements is CORRECT?
    A. Only Sentence I is written in correct English.
    B. Only Sentence II is written in correct English.
    C. Sentences I and II are both written in correct English.
    D. Neither Sentence I nor Sentence II is written in correct English.

15._____

16. Following are two sentences which may or may not be written in correct English:					16.____
    I. Officer McElroy putted out a small fire in the wastepaper basket.
    II. Special Officer Janssen told the visitor where he could obtained a pass.
   Which one of the following statements is CORRECT?
      A. Only Sentence I is written in correct English.
      B. Only Sentence II is written in correct English.
      C. Sentences I and II are both written in correct English.
      D. Neither Sentence I nor Sentence II is written in correct English.

17. Following are two sentences which may or may not be written in correct English:					17.____
    I. Security Officer Warren observed a broken window while he was on his post in Hallway C.
    II. The worker reported that two typewriters had been stolen from the office,
   Which one of the following statements is CORRECT?
      A. Only Sentence I is written in correct English.
      B. Only Sentence II is written in correct English.
      C. Sentences I and II are both written in correct English.
      D. Neither Sentence I nor Sentence II is written in correct English,

18. Following are two sentences which may or may not be written in correct English:					18.____
    I. Special Officer Cleveland was attempting to calm an emotionally disturbed visitor.
    II. The visitor did not stop crying and calling for his wife.
   Which one of the following statements is CORRECT?
      A. Only Sentence I is written in correct English.
      B. Only Sentence II is written in correct English.
      C. Sentences I and II are both written in correct English.
      D. Neither Sentence I nor Sentence II is written in correct English.

19. Following are two sentences that may or may not be written in correct English:					19.____
    I. While on patrol, I observes a vagrant loitering near the drug dispensary.
    II. I escorted the vagrant out of the building and off the premises.
   Which one of the following statements is CORRECT?
      A. Only Sentence I is written in correct English.
      B. Only Sentence II is written in correct English.
      C. Sentences I and II are both written in correct English.
      D. Neither Sentence I nor Sentence II is written in correct English.

20. Following are two sentences which may or may not be written in correct English:					20.____
    I. At 4:00 P.M., Sergeant Raymond told me to evacuate the waiting area immediately due to a bomb threat.
    II. Some of the clients did not want to leave the building.
   Which one of the following statements is CORRECT?
      A. Only Sentence I is written in correct English.
      B. Only Sentence II is written in correct English.
      C. Sentences I and II are both written in correct English.
      D. Neither Sentence I nor Sentence II is written in correct English.

KEY (CORRECT ANSWERS)

1. B 11. A
2. A 12. C
3. C 13. D
4. D 14. C
5. A 15. A

6. C 16. D
7. B 17. A
8. D 18. A
9. C 19. B
10. A 20. C

GLOSSARY OF LEGAL TERMS

TABLE OF CONTENTS

	Page
Action ... Affiant	1
Affidavit ... At Bar	2
At Issue ... Burden of Proof	3
Business ... Commute	4
Complainant ... Conviction	5
Cooperative ... Demur (v.)	6
Demurrage ... Endorsement	7
Enjoin ... Facsimile	8
Factor ... Guilty	9
Habeas Corpus ... Incumbrance	10
Indemnify ... Laches	11
Landlord and Tenant ... Malice	12
Mandamus ... Obiter Dictum	13
Object (v.) ... Perjury	14
Perpetuity ... Proclamation	15
Proffered Evidence ... Referee	16
Referendum ... Stare Decisis	17
State ... Term	18
Testamentary ... Warrant (Warranty) (v.)	19
Warrant (n.) ... Zoning	20

GLOSSARY OF LEGAL TERMS

A

ACTION - "Action" includes a civil action and a criminal action.

A FORTIORI - A term meaning you can reason one thing from the existence of certain facts.

A POSTERIORI - From what goes after; from effect to cause.

A PRIORI - From what goes before; from cause to effect.

AB INITIO - From the beginning.

ABATE - To diminish or put an end to.

ABET - To encourage the commission of a crime.

ABEYANCE - Suspension, temporary suppression.

ABIDE - To accept the consequences of.

ABJURE - To renounce; give up.

ABRIDGE - To reduce; contract; diminish.

ABROGATE - To annul, repeal, or destroy.

ABSCOND - To hide or absent oneself to avoid legal action.

ABSTRACT - A summary.

ABUT - To border on, to touch.

ACCESS - Approach; in real property law it means the right of the owner of property to the use of the highway or road next to his land, without obstruction by intervening property owners.

ACCESSORY - In criminal law, it means the person who contributes or aids in the commission of a crime.

ACCOMMODATED PARTY - One to whom credit is extended on the strength of another person signing a commercial paper.

ACCOMMODATION PAPER - A commercial paper to which the accommodating party has put his name.

ACCOMPLICE - In criminal law, it means a person who together with the principal offender commits a crime.

ACCORD - An agreement to accept something different or less than that to which one is entitled, which extinguishes the entire obligation.

ACCOUNT - A statement of mutual demands in the nature of debt and credit between parties.

ACCRETION - The act of adding to a thing; in real property law, it means gradual accumulation of land by natural causes.

ACCRUE - To grow to; to be added to.

ACKNOWLEDGMENT - The act of going before an official authorized to take acknowledgments, and acknowledging an act as one's own.

ACQUIESCENCE - A silent appearance of consent.

ACQUIT - To legally determine the innocence of one charged with a crime.

AD INFINITUM - Indefinitely.

AD LITEM - For the suit.

AD VALOREM - According to value.

ADJECTIVE LAW - Rules of procedure.

ADJUDICATION - The judgment given in a case.

ADMIRALTY - Court having jurisdiction over maritime cases.

ADULT - Sixteen years old or over (in criminal law).

ADVANCE - In commercial law, it means to pay money or render other value before it is due.

ADVERSE - Opposed; contrary.

ADVOCATE - (v.) To speak in favor of;
             (n.) One who assists, defends, or pleads for another.

AFFIANT - A person who makes and signs an affidavit.

AFFIDAVIT - A written and sworn to declaration of facts, voluntarily made.
AFFINITY- The relationship between persons through marriage with the kindred of each other; distinguished from consanguinity, which is the relationship by blood.
AFFIRM - To ratify; also when an appellate court affirms a judgment, decree, or order, it means that it is valid and right and must stand as rendered in the lower court.
AFOREMENTIONED; AFORESAID - Before or already said.
AGENT - One who represents and acts for another.
AID AND COMFORT - To help; encourage.
ALIAS - A name not one's true name.
ALIBI - A claim of not being present at a certain place at a certain time.
ALLEGE - To assert.
ALLOTMENT - A share or portion.
AMBIGUITY - Uncertainty; capable of being understood in more than one way.
AMENDMENT - Any language made or proposed as a change in some principal writing.
AMICUS CURIAE - A friend of the court; one who has an interest in a case, although not a party in the case, who volunteers advice upon matters of law to the judge. For example, a brief amicus curiae.
AMORTIZATION - To provide for a gradual extinction of (a future obligation) in advance of maturity, especially, by periodical contributions to a sinking fund which will be adequate to discharge a debt or make a replacement when it becomes necessary.
ANCILLARY - Aiding, auxiliary.
ANNOTATION - A note added by way of comment or explanation.
ANSWER - A written statement made by a defendant setting forth the grounds of his defense.
ANTE - Before.
ANTE MORTEM - Before death.
APPEAL - The removal of a case from a lower court to one of superior jurisdiction for the purpose of obtaining a review.
APPEARANCE - Coming into court as a party to a suit.
APPELLANT - The party who takes an appeal from one court or jurisdiction to another (appellate) court for review.
APPELLEE - The party against whom an appeal is taken.
APPROPRIATE - To make a thing one's own.
APPROPRIATION - Prescribing the destination of a thing; the act of the legislature designating a particular fund, to be applied to some object of government expenditure.
APPURTENANT - Belonging to; accessory or incident to.
ARBITER - One who decides a dispute; a referee.
ARBITRARY - Unreasoned; not governed by any fixed rules or standard.
ARGUENDO - By way of argument.
ARRAIGN - To call the prisoner before the court to answer to a charge.
ASSENT - A declaration of willingness to do something in compliance with a request.
ASSERT - Declare.
ASSESS - To fix the rate or amount.
ASSIGN - To transfer; to appoint; to select for a particular purpose.
ASSIGNEE - One who receives an assignment.
ASSIGNOR - One who makes an assignment.
AT BAR - Before the court.

AT ISSUE - When parties in an action come to a point where one asserts something and the other denies it.
ATTACH - Seize property by court order and sometimes arrest a person.
ATTEST - To witness a will, etc.; act of attestation.
AVERMENT - A positive statement of facts.

B

BAIL - To obtain the release of a person from legal custody by giving security and promising that he shall appear in court; to deliver (goods, etc.) in trust to a person for a special purpose.
BAILEE - One to whom personal property is delivered under a contract of bailment.
BAILMENT - Delivery of personal property to another to be held for a certain purpose and to be returned when the purpose is accomplished.
BAILOR - The party who delivers goods to another, under a contract of bailment.
BANC (OR BANK) - Bench; the place where a court sits permanently or regularly; also the assembly of all the judges of a court.
BANKRUPT - An insolvent person, technically, one declared to be bankrupt after a bankruptcy proceeding.
BAR - The legal profession.
BARRATRY - Exciting groundless judicial proceedings.
BARTER - A contract by which parties exchange goods for other goods.
BATTERY - Illegal interfering with another's person.
BEARER - In commercial law, it means the person in possession of a commercial paper which is payable to the bearer.
BENCH - The court itself or the judge.
BENEFICIARY - A person benefiting under a will, trust, or agreement.
BEST EVIDENCE RULE,THE - Except as otherwise provided by statute, no evidence other than the writing itself is admissible to prove the content of a writing. This section shall be known and may be cited as the best evidence rule.
BEQUEST - A gift of personal property under a will.
BILL - A formal written statement of complaint to a court of justice; also, a draft of an act of the legislature before it becomes a law; also, accounts for goods sold, services rendered, or work done.
BONA FIDE - In or with good faith; honestly.
BOND - An instrument by which the maker promises to pay a sum of money to another, usually providing that upon performances of a certain condition the obligation shall be void.
BOYCOTT - A plan to prevent the carrying on of a business by wrongful means.
BREACH - The breaking or violating of a law, or the failure to carry out a duty.
BRIEF - A written document, prepared by a lawyer to serve as the basis of an argument upon a case in court, usually an appellate court.
BURDEN OF PRODUCING EVIDENCE - The obligation of a party to introduce evidence sufficient to avoid a ruling against him on the issue.
BURDEN OF PROOF - The obligation of a party to establish by evidence a requisite degree of belief concerning a fact in the mind of the trier of fact or the court. The burden of proof may require a party to raise a reasonable doubt concerning the existence of nonexistence of a fact or that he establish the existence or nonexistence of a fact by a preponderance of the evidence, by clear and convincing proof, or by proof beyond a reasonable doubt.

Except as otherwise provided by law, the burden of proof requires proof by a preponderance of the evidence.

BUSINESS, A - Shall include every kind of business, profession, occupation, calling or operation of institutions, whether carried on for profit or not.

BY-LAWS - Regulations, ordinances, or rules enacted by a corporation, association, etc., for its own government.

C

CANON - A doctrine; also, a law or rule, of a church or association in particular.

CAPIAS - An order to arrest.

CAPTION - In a pleading, deposition or other paper connected with a case in court, it is the heading or introductory clause which shows the names of the parties, name of the court, number of the case on the docket or calendar, etc.

CARRIER - A person or corporation undertaking to transport persons or property.

CASE - A general term for an action, cause, suit, or controversy before a judicial body.

CAUSE - A suit, litigation or action before a court.

CAVEAT EMPTOR - Let the buyer beware. This term expresses the rule that the purchaser of an article must examine, judge, and test it for himself, being bound to discover any obvious defects or imperfections.

CERTIFICATE - A written representation that some legal formality has been complied with.

CERTIORARI - To be informed of; the name of a writ issued by a superior court directing the lower court to send up to the former the record and proceedings of a case.

CHANGE OF VENUE - To remove place of trial from one place to another.

CHARGE - An obligation or duty; a formal complaint; an instruction of the court to the jury upon a case.

CHARTER - (n.) The authority by virtue of which an organized body acts;
   (v.) in mercantile law, it means to hire or lease a vehicle or vessel for transportation.

CHATTEL - An article of personal property.

CHATTEL MORTGAGE - A mortgage on personal property.

CIRCUIT - A division of the country, for the administration of justice; a geographical area served by a court.

CITATION - The act of the court by which a person is summoned or cited; also, a reference to legal authority.

CIVIL (ACTIONS)- It indicates the private rights and remedies of individuals in contrast to the word "criminal" (actions) which relates to prosecution for violation of laws.

CLAIM (n.) - Any demand held or asserted as of right.

CODICIL - An addition to a will.

CODIFY - To arrange the laws of a country into a code.

COGNIZANCE - Notice or knowledge.

COLLATERAL - By the side; accompanying; an article or thing given to secure performance of a promise.

COMITY - Courtesy; the practice by which one court follows the decision of another court on the same question.

COMMIT - To perform, as an act; to perpetrate, as a crime; to send a person to prison.

COMMON LAW - As distinguished from law created by the enactment of the legislature (called statutory law), it relates to those principles and rules of action which derive their authority solely from usages and customs of immemorial antiquity, particularly with reference to the ancient unwritten law of England. The written pronouncements of the common law are found in court decisions.

COMMUTE - Change punishment to one less severe.

COMPLAINANT - One who applies to the court for legal redress.
COMPLAINT - The pleading of a plaintiff in a civil action; or a charge that a person has committed a specified offense.
COMPROMISE - An arrangement for settling a dispute by agreement.
CONCUR - To agree, consent.
CONCURRENT - Running together, at the same time.
CONDEMNATION - Taking private property for public use on payment therefor.
CONDITION - Mode or state of being; a qualification or restriction.
CONDUCT - Active and passive behavior; both verbal and nonverbal.
CONFESSION - Voluntary statement of guilt of crime.
CONFIDENTIAL COMMUNICATION BETWEEN CLIENT AND LAWYER - Information transmitted between a client and his lawyer in the course of that relationship and in confidence by a means which, so far as the client is aware, discloses the information to no third persons other than those who are present to further the interest of the client in the consultation or those to whom disclosure is reasonably necessary for the transmission of the information or the accomplishment of the purpose for which the lawyer is consulted, and includes a legal opinion formed and the advice given by the lawyer in the course of that relationship.
CONFRONTATION - Witness testifying in presence of defendant.
CONSANGUINITY - Blood relationship.
CONSIGN - To give in charge; commit; entrust; to send or transmit goods to a merchant, factor, or agent for sale.
CONSIGNEE - One to whom a consignment is made.
CONSIGNOR - One who sends or makes a consignment.
CONSPIRACY - In criminal law, it means an agreement between two or more persons to commit an unlawful act.
CONSPIRATORS - Persons involved in a conspiracy.
CONSTITUTION - The fundamental law of a nation or state.
CONSTRUCTION OF GENDERS - The masculine gender includes the feminine and neuter.
CONSTRUCTION OF SINGULAR AND PLURAL - The singular number includes the plural; and the plural, the singular.
CONSTRUCTION OF TENSES - The present tense includes the past and future tenses; and the future, the present.
CONSTRUCTIVE - An act or condition assumed from other parts or conditions.
CONSTRUE - To ascertain the meaning of language.
CONSUMMATE - To complete.
CONTIGUOUS - Adjoining; touching; bounded by.
CONTINGENT - Possible, but not assured; dependent upon some condition.
CONTINUANCE - The adjournment or postponement of an action pending in a court.
CONTRA - Against, opposed to; contrary.
CONTRACT - An agreement between two or more persons to do or not to do a particular thing.
CONTROVERT - To dispute, deny.
CONVERSION - Dealing with the personal property of another as if it were one's own, without right.
CONVEYANCE - An instrument transferring title to land.
CONVICTION - Generally, the result of a criminal trial which ends in a judgment or sentence that the defendant is guilty as charged.

COOPERATIVE - A cooperative is a voluntary organization of persons with a common interest, formed and operated along democratic lines for the purpose of supplying services at cost to its members and other patrons, who contribute both capital and business.

CORPUS DELICTI - The body of a crime; the crime itself.

CORROBORATE - To strengthen; to add weight by additional evidence.

COUNTERCLAIM - A claim presented by a defendant in opposition to or deduction from the claim of the plaintiff.

COUNTY - Political subdivision of a state.

COVENANT - Agreement.

CREDIBLE - Worthy of belief.

CREDITOR - A person to whom a debt is owing by another person, called the "debtor."

CRIMINAL ACTION - Includes criminal proceedings.

CRIMINAL INFORMATION - Same as complaint.

CRITERION (sing.)

CRITERIA (plural) - A means or tests for judging; a standard or standards.

CROSS-EXAMINATION - Examination of a witness by a party other than the direct examiner upon a matter that is within the scope of the direct examination of the witness.

CULPABLE - Blamable.

CY-PRES - As near as (possible). The rule of *cy-pres* is a rule for the construction of instruments in equity by which the intention of the party is carried out *as near as may be*, when it would be impossible or illegal to give it literal effect.

D

DAMAGES - A monetary compensation, which may be recovered in the courts by any person who has suffered loss, or injury, whether to his person, property or rights through the unlawful act or omission or negligence of another.

DECLARANT - A person who makes a statement.

DE FACTO - In fact; actually but without legal authority.

DE JURE - Of right; legitimate; lawful.

DE MINIMIS - Very small or trifling.

DE NOVO - Anew; afresh; a second time.

DEBT - A specified sum of money owing to one person from another, including not only the obligation of the debtor to pay, but the right of the creditor to receive and enforce payment.

DECEDENT - A dead person.

DECISION - A judgment or decree pronounced by a court in determination of a case.

DECREE - An order of the court, determining the rights of all parties to a suit.

DEED - A writing containing a contract sealed and delivered; particularly to convey real property.

DEFALCATION - Misappropriation of funds.

DEFAMATION - Injuring one's reputation by false statements.

DEFAULT - The failure to fulfill a duty, observe a promise, discharge an obligation, or perform an agreement.

DEFENDANT - The person defending or denying; the party against whom relief or recovery is sought in an action or suit.

DEFRAUD - To practice fraud; to cheat or trick.

DELEGATE (v.)- To entrust to the care or management of another.

DELICTUS - A crime.

DEMUR (v.) - To dispute the sufficiency in law of the pleading of the other side.

DEMURRAGE - In maritime law, it means, the sum fixed or allowed as remuneration to the owners of a ship for the detention of their vessel beyond the number of days allowed for loading and unloading or for sailing; also used in railroad terminology.
DENIAL - A form of pleading; refusing to admit the truth of a statement, charge, etc.
DEPONENT - One who gives testimony under oath reduced to writing.
DEPOSITION - Testimony given under oath outside of court for use in court or for the purpose of obtaining information in preparation for trial of a case.
DETERIORATION - A degeneration such as from decay, corrosion or disintegration.
DETRIMENT - Any loss or harm to person or property.
DEVIATION - A turning aside.
DEVISE - A gift of real property by the last will and testament of the donor.
DICTUM (sing.)
DICTA (plural) - Any statements made by the court in an opinion concerning some rule of law not necessarily involved nor essential to the determination of the case.
DIRECT EVIDENCE - Evidence that directly proves a fact, without an inference or presumption, and which in itself if true, conclusively establishes that fact.
DIRECT EXAMINATION - The first examination of a witness upon a matter that is not within the scope of a previous examination of the witness.
DISAFFIRM - To repudiate.
DISMISS - In an action or suit, it means to dispose of the case without any further consideration or hearing.
DISSENT - To denote disagreement of one or more judges of a court with the decision passed by the majority upon a case before them.
DOCKET (n.) - A formal record, entered in brief, of the proceedings in a court.
DOCTRINE - A rule, principle, theory of law.
DOMICILE - That place where a man has his true, fixed and permanent home to which whenever he is absent he has the intention of returning.
DRAFT (n.) - A commercial paper ordering payment of money drawn by one person on another.
DRAWEE - The person who is requested to pay the money.
DRAWER - The person who draws the commercial paper and addresses it to the drawee.
DUPLICATE - A counterpart produced by the same impression as the original enlargements and miniatures, or by mechanical or electronic re-recording, or by chemical reproduction, or by other equivalent technique which accurately reproduces the original.
DURESS - Use of force to compel performance or non-performance of an act.

E

EASEMENT - A liberty, privilege, or advantage without profit, in the lands of another.
EGRESS - Act or right of going out or leaving; emergence.
EIUSDEM GENERIS - Of the same kind, class or nature. A rule used in the construction of language in a legal document.
EMBEZZLEMENT - To steal; to appropriate fraudulently to one's own use property entrusted to one's care.
EMBRACERY - Unlawful attempt to influence jurors, etc., but not by offering value.
EMINENT DOMAIN - The right of a state to take private property for public use.
ENACT - To make into a law.
ENDORSEMENT - Act of writing one's name on the back of a note, bill or similar written instrument.

ENJOIN - To require a person, by writ of injunction from a court of equity, to perform or to abstain or desist from some act.
ENTIRETY - The whole; that which the law considers as one whole, and not capable of being divided into parts.
ENTRAPMENT - Inducing one to commit a crime so as to arrest him.
ENUMERATED - Mentioned specifically; designated.
ENURE - To operate or take effect.
EQUITY - In its broadest sense, this term denotes the spirit and the habit of fairness, justness, and right dealing which regulate the conduct of men.
ERROR - A mistake of law, or the false or irregular application of law as will nullify the judicial proceedings.
ESCROW - A deed, bond or other written engagement, delivered to a third person, to be delivered by him only upon the performance or fulfillment of some condition.
ESTATE - The interest which any one has in lands, or in any other subject of property.
ESTOP - To stop, bar, or impede.
ESTOPPEL - A rule of law which prevents a man from alleging or denying a fact, because of his own previous act.
ET AL. (alii) - And others.
ET SEQ. (sequential) - And the following.
ET UX. (uxor) - And wife.
EVIDENCE - Testimony, writings, material objects, or other things presented to the senses that are offered to prove the existence or non-existence of a fact.
   Means from which inferences may be drawn as a basis of proof in duly constituted judicial or fact finding tribunals, and includes testimony in the form of opinion and hearsay.
EX CONTRACTU
EX DELICTO - In law, rights and causes of action are divided into two classes, those arising *ex contractu* (from a contract) and those arising *ex delicto* (from a delict or tort).
EX OFFICIO - From office; by virtue of the office.
EX PARTE - On one side only; by or for one.
EX POST FACTO - After the fact.
EX POST FACTO LAW - A law passed after an act was done which retroactively makes such act a crime.
EX REL. (relations) - Upon relation or information.
EXCEPTION - An objection upon a matter of law to a decision made, either before or after judgment by a court.
EXECUTOR (male)
EXECUTRIX (female) - A person who has been appointed by will to execute the will.
EXECUTORY - That which is yet to be executed or performed.
EXEMPT - To release from some liability to which others are subject.
EXONERATION - The removal of a burden, charge or duty.
EXTRADITION - Surrender of a fugitive from one nation to another.

F

F.A.S.- "Free alongside ship"; delivery at dock for ship named.
F.O.B.- "Free on board"; seller will deliver to car, truck, vessel, or other conveyance by which goods are to be transported, without expense or risk of loss to the buyer or consignee.
FABRICATE - To construct; to invent a false story.
FACSIMILE - An exact or accurate copy of an original instrument.

FACTOR - A commercial agent.
FEASANCE - The doing of an act.
FELONIOUS - Criminal, malicious.
FELONY - Generally, a criminal offense that may be punished by death or imprisonment for more than one year as differentiated from a misdemeanor.
FEME SOLE - A single woman.
FIDUCIARY - A person who is invested with rights and powers to be exercised for the benefit of another person.
FIERI FACIAS - A writ of execution commanding the sheriff to levy and collect the amount of a judgment from the goods and chattels of the judgment debtor.
FINDING OF FACT - Determination from proof or judicial notice of the existence of a fact. A ruling implies a supporting finding of fact; no separate or formal finding is required unless required by a statute of this state.
FISCAL - Relating to accounts or the management of revenue.
FORECLOSURE (sale) - A sale of mortgaged property to obtain satisfaction of the mortgage out of the sale proceeds.
FORFEITURE - A penalty, a fine.
FORGERY - Fabricating or producing falsely, counterfeited.
FORTUITOUS - Accidental.
FORUM - A court of justice; a place of jurisdiction.
FRAUD - Deception; trickery.
FREEHOLDER - One who owns real property.
FUNGIBLE - Of such kind or nature that one specimen or part may be used in the place of another.

G

GARNISHEE - Person garnished.
GARNISHMENT - A legal process to reach the money or effects of a defendant, in the possession or control of a third person.
GRAND JURY - Not less than 16, not more than 23 citizens of a county sworn to inquire into crimes committed or triable in the county.
GRANT - To agree to; convey, especially real property.
GRANTEE - The person to whom a grant is made.
GRANTOR - The person by whom a grant is made.
GRATUITOUS - Given without a return, compensation or consideration.
GRAVAMEN - The grievance complained of or the substantial cause of a criminal action.
GUARANTY (n.) - A promise to answer for the payment of some debt, or the performance of some duty, in case of the failure of another person, who, in the first instance, is liable for such payment or performance.
GUARDIAN - The person, committee, or other representative authorized by law to protect the person or estate or both of an incompetent (or of a *sui juris* person having a guardian) and to act for him in matters affecting his person or property or both. An incompetent is a person under disability imposed by law.
GUILTY - Establishment of the fact that one has committed a breach of conduct; especially, a violation of law.

H

HABEAS CORPUS - You have the body; the name given to a variety of writs, having for their object to bring a party before a court or judge for decision as to whether such person is being lawfully held prisoner.

HABENDUM - In conveyancing; it is the clause in a deed conveying land which defines the extent of ownership to be held by the grantee.

HEARING - A proceeding whereby the arguments of the interested parties are heared.

HEARSAY - A type of testimony given by a witness who relates, not what he knows personally, but what others have told hi, or what he has heard said by others.

HEARSAY RULE, THE - (a) "Hearsay evidence" is evidence of a statement that was made other than by a witness while testifying at the hearing and that is offered to prove the truth of the matter stated; (b) Except as provided by law, hearsay evidence is inadmissible; (c) This section shall be known and may be cited as the hearsay rule.

HEIR - Generally, one who inherits property, real or personal.

HOLDER OF THE PRIVILEGE - (a) The client when he has no guardian or conservator; (b) A guardian or conservator of the client when the client has a guardian or conservator; (c) The personal representative of the client if the client is dead; (d) A successor, assign, trustee in dissolution, or any similar representative of a firm, association, organization, partnership, business trust, corporation, or public entity that is no longer in existence.

HUNG JURY - One so divided that they can't agree on a verdict.

HUSBAND-WIFE PRIVILEGE - An accused in a criminal proceeding has a privilege to prevent his spouse from testifying against him.

HYPOTHECATE - To pledge a thing without delivering it to the pledgee.

HYPOTHESIS - A supposition, assumption, or toehry.

I

I.E. (id est) - That is.

IB., OR IBID.(ibidem) - In the same place; used to refer to a legal reference previously cited to avoid repeating the entire citation.

ILLICIT - Prohibited; unlawful.

ILLUSORY - Deceiving by false appearance.

IMMUNITY - Exemption.

IMPEACH - To accuse, to dispute.

IMPEDIMENTS - Disabilities, or hindrances.

IMPLEAD - To sue or prosecute by due course of law.

IMPUTED - Attributed or charged to.

IN LOCO PARENTIS - In place of parent, a guardian.

IN TOTO - In the whole; completely.

INCHOATE - Imperfect; unfinished.

INCOMMUNICADO - Denial of the right of a prisoner to communicate with friends or relatives.

INCOMPETENT - One who is incapable of caring for his own affairs because he is mentally deficient or undeveloped.

INCRIMINATION - A matter will incriminate a person if it constitutes, or forms an essential part of, or, taken in connection with other matters disclosed, is a basis for a reasonable inference of such a violation of the laws of this State as to subject him to liability to punishment therefor, unless he has become for any reason permanently immune from punishment for such violation.

INCUMBRANCE - Generally a claim, lien, charge or liability attached to and binding real property.

INDEMNIFY - To secure against loss or damage; also, to make reimbursement to one for a loss already incurred by him.
INDEMNITY - An agreement to reimburse another person in case of an anticipated loss falling upon him.
INDICIA - Signs; indications.
INDICTMENT - An accusation in writing found and presented by a grand jury charging that a person has committed a crime.
INDORSE - To write a name on the back of a legal paper or document, generally, a negotiable instrument
INDUCEMENT - Cause or reason why a thing is done or that which incites the person to do the act or commit a crime; the motive for the criminal act.
INFANT - In civil cases one under 21 years of age.
INFORMATION - A formal accusation of crime made by a prosecuting attorney.
INFRA - Below, under; this word occurring by itself in a publication refers the reader to a future part of the publication.
INGRESS - The act of going into.
INJUNCTION - A writ or order by the court requiring a person, generally, to do or to refrain from doing an act.
INSOLVENT - The condition of a person who is unable to pay his debts.
INSTRUCTION - A direction given by the judge to the jury concerning the law of the case.
INTERIM - In the meantime; time intervening.
INTERLOCUTORY - Temporary, not final; something intervening between the commencement and the end of a suit which decides some point or matter, but is not a final decision of the whole controversy.
INTERROGATORIES - A series of formal written questions used in the examination of a party or a witness usually prior to a trial.
INTESTATE - A person who dies without a will.
INURE - To result, to take effect.
IPSO FACTO - By the fact iself; by the mere fact.
ISSUE (n.) The disputed point or question in a case,

J

JEOPARDY - Danger, hazard, peril.
JOINDER - Joining; uniting with another person in some legal steps or proceeding.
JOINT - United; combined.
JUDGE - Member or members or representative or representatives of a court conducting a trial or hearing at which evidence is introduced.
JUDGMENT - The official decision of a court of justice.
JUDICIAL OR JUDICIARY - Relating to or connected with the administration of justice.
JURAT - The clause written at the foot of an affidavit, stating when, where and before whom such affidavit was sworn.
JURISDICTION - The authority to hear and determine controversies between parties.
JURISPRUDENCE - The philosophy of law.
JURY - A body of persons legally selected to inquire into any matter of fact, and to render their verdict according to the evidence.

L

LACHES - The failure to diligently assert a right, which results in a refusal to allow relief.

LANDLORD AND TENANT - A phrase used to denote the legal relation existing between the owner and occupant of real estate.

LARCENY - Stealing personal property belonging to another.

LATENT - Hidden; that which does not appear on the face of a thing.

LAW - Includes constitutional, statutory, and decisional law.

LAWYER-CLIENT PRIVILEGE - (1) A "client" is a person, public officer, or corporation, association, or other organization or entity, either public or private, who is rendered professional legal services by a lawyer, or who consults a lawyer with a view to obtaining professional legal services from him; (2) A "lawyer" is a person authorized, or reasonably believed by the client to be authorized, to practice law in any state or nation; (3) A "representative of the lawyer" is one employed to assist the lawyer in the rendition of professional legal services; (4) A communication is "confidential" if not intended to be disclosed to third persons other than those to whom disclosure is in furtherance of the rendition of professional legal services to the client or those reasonably necessary for the transmission of the communication.

General rule of privilege - A client has a privilege to refuse to disclose and to prevent any other person from disclosing confidential communications made for the purpose of facilitating the rendition of professional legal services to the client, (1) between himself or his representative and his lawyer or his lawyer's representative, or (2) between his lawyer and the lawyer's representative, or (3) by him or his lawyer to a lawyer representing another in a matter of common interest, or (4) between representatives of the client or between the client and a representative of the client, or (5) between lawyers representing the client.

LEADING QUESTION - Question that suggests to the witness the answer that the examining party desires.

LEASE - A contract by which one conveys real estate for a limited time usually for a specified rent; personal property also may be leased.

LEGISLATION - The act of enacting laws.

LEGITIMATE - Lawful.

LESSEE - One to whom a lease is given.

LESSOR - One who grants a lease

LEVY - A collecting or exacting by authority.

LIABLE - Responsible; bound or obligated in law or equity.

LIBEL (v.) - To defame or injure a person's reputation by a published writing.

(n.) - The initial pleading on the part of the plaintiff in an admiralty proceeding.

LIEN - A hold or claim which one person has upon the property of another as a security for some debt or charge.

LIQUIDATED - Fixed; settled.

LIS PENDENS - A pending civil or criminal action.

LITERAL - According to the language.

LITIGANT - A party to a lawsuit.

LITATION - A judicial controversy.

LOCUS - A place.

LOCUS DELICTI - Place of the crime.

LOCUS POENITENTIAE - The abandoning or giving up of one's intention to commit some crime before it is fully completed or abandoning a conspiracy before its purpose is accomplished.

M

MALFEASANCE - To do a wrongful act.

MALICE - The doing of a wrongful act Intentionally without just cause or excuse.

MANDAMUS - The name of a writ issued by a court to enforce the performance of some public duty.
MANDATORY (adj.) Containing a command.
MARITIME - Pertaining to the sea or to commerce thereon.
MARSHALING - Arranging or disposing of in order.
MAXIM - An established principle or proposition.
MINISTERIAL - That which involves obedience to instruction, but demands no special discretion, judgment or skill.
MISAPPROPRIATE - Dealing fraudulently with property entrusted to one.
MISDEMEANOR - A crime less than a felony and punishable by a fine or imprisonment for less than one year.
MISFEASANCE - Improper performance of a lawful act.
MISREPRESENTATION - An untrue representation of facts.
MITIGATE - To make or become less severe, harsh.
MITTIMUS - A warrant of commitment to prison.
MOOT (adj.) Unsettled, undecided, not necessary to be decided.
MORTGAGE - A conveyance of property upon condition, as security for the payment of a debt or the performance of a duty, and to become void upon payment or performance according to the stipulated terms.
MORTGAGEE - A person to whom property is mortgaged.
MORTGAGOR - One who gives a mortgage.
MOTION - In legal proceedings, a "motion" is an application, either written or oral, addressed to the court by a party to an action or a suit requesting the ruling of the court on a matter of law.
MUTUALITY - Reciprocation.

N

NEGLIGENCE - The failure to exercise that degree of care which an ordinarily prudent person would exercise under like circumstances.
NEGOTIABLE (instrument) - Any instrument obligating the payment of money which is transferable from one person to another by endorsement and delivery or by delivery only.
NEGOTIATE - To transact business; to transfer a negotiable instrument; to seek agreement for the amicable disposition of a controversy or case.
NOLLE PROSEQUI - A formal entry upon the record, by the plaintiff in a civil suit or the prosecuting officer in a criminal action, by which he declares that he "will no further prosecute" the case.
NOLO CONTENDERE - The name of a plea in a criminal action, having the same effect as a plea of guilty; but not constituting a direct admission of guilt.
NOMINAL - Not real or substantial.
NOMINAL DAMAGES - Award of a trifling sum where no substantial injury is proved to have been sustained.
NONFEASANCE - Neglect of duty.
NOVATION - The substitution of a new debt or obligation for an existing one.
NUNC PRO TUNC - A phrase applied to acts allowed to be done after the time when they should be done, with a retroactive effect.("Now for then.")

O

OATH - Oath includes affirmation or declaration under penalty of perjury.
OBITER DICTUM - Opinion expressed by a court on a matter not essentially involved in a case and hence not a decision; also called dicta, if plural.

OBJECT (v.) - To oppose as improper or illegal and referring the question of its propriety or legality to the court.
OBLIGATION - A legal duty, by which a person is bound to do or not to do a certain thing.
OBLIGEE - The person to whom an obligation is owed.
OBLIGOR - The person who is to perform the obligation.
OFFER (v.) - To present for acceptance or rejection.
    (n.) - A proposal to do a thing, usually a proposal to make a contract.
OFFICIAL INFORMATION - Information within the custody or control of a department or agency of the government the disclosure of which is shown to be contrary to the public interest.
OFFSET - A deduction.
ONUS PROBANDI - Burden of proof.
OPINION - The statement by a judge of the decision reached in a case, giving the law as applied to the case and giving reasons for the judgment; also a belief or view.
OPTION - The exercise of the power of choice; also a privilege existing in one person, for which he has paid money, which gives him the right to buy or sell real or personal property at a given price within a specified time.
ORDER - A rule or regulation; every direction of a court or judge made or entered in writing but not including a judgment.
ORDINANCE - Generally, a rule established by authority; also commonly used to designate the legislative acts of a municipal corporation.
ORIGINAL - Writing or recording itself or any counterpart intended to have the same effect by a person executing or issuing it. An "original" of a photograph includes the negative or any print therefrom. If data are stored in a computer or similar device, any printout or other output readable by sight, shown to reflect the data accurately, is an "original."
OVERT - Open, manifest.

P

PANEL - A group of jurors selected to serve during a term of the court.
PARENS PATRIAE - Sovereign power of a state to protect or be a guardian over children and incompetents.
PAROL - Oral or verbal.
PAROLE - To release one in prison before the expiration of his sentence, conditionally.
PARITY - Equality in purchasing power between the farmer and other segments of the economy.
PARTITION - A legal division of real or personal property between one or more owners.
PARTNERSHIP - An association of two or more persons to carry on as co-owners a business for profit.
PATENT (adj.) - Evident.
    (n.) - A grant of some privilege, property, or authority, made by the government or sovereign of a country to one or more individuals.
PECULATION - Stealing.
PECUNIARY - Monetary.
PENULTIMATE - Next to the last.
PER CURIAM - A phrase used in the report of a decision to distinguish an opinion of the whole court from an opinion written by any one judge.
PER SE - In itself; taken alone.
PERCEIVE - To acquire knowledge through one's senses.
PEREMPTORY - Imperative; absolute.
PERJURY - To lie or state falsely under oath.

PERPETUITY - Perpetual existence; also the quality or condition of an estate limited so that it will not take effect or vest within the period fixed by law.
PERSON - Includes a natural person, firm, association, organization, partnership, business trust, corporation, or public entity.
PERSONAL PROPERTY - Includes money, goods, chattels, things in action, and evidences of debt.
PERSONALTY - Short term for personal property.
PETITION - An application in writing for an order of the court, stating the circumstances upon which it is founded and requesting any order or other relief from a court.
PLAINTIFF - A person who brings a court action.
PLEA - A pleading in a suit or action.
PLEADINGS - Formal allegations made by the parties of their respective claims and defenses, for the judgment of the court.
PLEDGE - A deposit of personal property as a security for the performance of an act.
PLEDGEE - The party to whom goods are delivered in pledge.
PLEDGOR - The party delivering goods in pledge.
PLENARY - Full; complete.
POLICE POWER - Inherent power of the state or its political subdivisions to enact laws within constitutional limits to promote the general welfare of society or the community.
POLLING THE JURY - Call the names of persons on a jury and requiring each juror to declare what his verdict is before it is legally recorded.
POST MORTEM - After death.
POWER OF ATTORNEY - A writing authorizing one to act for another.
PRECEPT - An order, warrant, or writ issued to an officer or body of officers, commanding him or them to do some act within the scope of his or their powers.
PRELIMINARY FACT - Fact upon the existence or nonexistence of which depends the admissibility or inadmissibility of evidence. The phrase "the admissibility or inadmissibility of evidence" includes the qualification or disqualification of a person to be a witness and the existence or nonexistence of a privilege.
PREPONDERANCE - Outweighing.
PRESENTMENT - A report by a grand jury on something they have investigated on their own knowledge.
PRESUMPTION - An assumption of fact resulting from a rule of law which requires such fact to be assumed from another fact or group of facts found or otherwise established in the action.
PRIMA FACUE - At first sight.
PRIMA FACIE CASE - A case where the evidence is very patent against the defendant.
PRINCIPAL - The source of authority or rights; a person primarily liable as differentiated from "principle" as a primary or basic doctrine.
PRO AND CON - For and against.
PRO RATA - Proportionally.
PROBATE - Relating to proof, especially to the proof of wills.
PROBATIVE - Tending to prove.
PROCEDURE - In law, this term generally denotes rules which are established by the Federal, State, or local Governments regarding the types of pleading and courtroom practice which must be followed by the parties involved in a criminal or civil case.
PROCLAMATION - A public notice by an official of some order, intended action, or state of facts.

PROFFERED EVIDENCE - The admissibility or inadmissibility of which is dependent upon the existence or nonexistence of a preliminary fact.
PROMISSORY (NOTE) - A promise in writing to pay a specified sum at an expressed time, or on demand, or at sight, to a named person, or to his order, or bearer.
PROOF - The establishment by evidence of a requisite degree of belief concerning a fact in the mind of the trier of fact or the court.
PROPERTY - Includes both real and personal property.
PROPRIETARY (adj.) - Relating or pertaining to ownership; usually a single owner.
PROSECUTE - To carry on an action or other judicial proceeding; to proceed against a person criminally.
PROVISO - A limitation or condition in a legal instrument.
PROXIMATE - Immediate; nearest
PUBLIC EMPLOYEE - An officer, agent, or employee of a public entity.
PUBLIC ENTITY - Includes a national, state, county, city and county, city, district, public authority, public agency, or any other political subdivision or public corporation, whether foreign or domestic.
PUBLIC OFFICIAL - Includes an official of a political dubdivision of such state or territory and of a municipality.
PUNITIVE - Relating to punishment.

Q

QUASH - To make void.
QUASI - As if; as it were.
QUID PRO QUO - Something for something; the giving of one valuable thing for another.
QUITCLAIM (v.) - To release or relinquish claim or title to, especially in deeds to realty.
QUO WARRANTO - A legal procedure to test an official's right to a public office or the right to hold a franchise, or to hold an office in a domestic corporation.

R

RATIFY - To approve and sanction.
REAL PROPERTY - Includes lands, tenements, and hereditaments.
REALTY - A brief term for real property.
REBUT - To contradict; to refute, especially by evidence and arguments.
RECEIVER - A person who is appointed by the court to receive, and hold in trust property in litigation.
RECIDIVIST - Habitual criminal.
RECIPROCAL - Mutual.
RECOUPMENT - To keep back or get something which is due; also, it is the right of a defendant to have a deduction from the amount of the plaintiff's damages because the plaintiff has not fulfilled his part of the same contract.
RECROSS EXAMINATION - Examination of a witness by a cross-examiner subsequent to a redirect examination of the witness.
REDEEM - To release an estate or article from mortgage or pledge by paying the debt for which it stood as security.
REDIRECT EXAMINATION - Examination of a witness by the direct examiner subsequent to the cross-examination of the witness.
REFEREE - A person to whom a cause pending in a court is referred by the court, to take testimony, hear the parties, and report thereon to the court.

REFERENDUM - A method of submitting an important legislative or administrative matter to a direct vote of the people.
RELEVANT EVIDENCE - Evidence including evidence relevant to the credulity of a witness or hearsay declarant, having any tendency in reason to prove or disprove any disputed fact that is of consequence to the determination of the action.
REMAND - To send a case back to the lower court from which it came, for further proceedings.
REPLEVIN - An action to recover goods or chattels wrongfully taken or detained.
REPLY (REPLICATION) - Generally, a reply is what the plaintiff or other person who has instituted proceedings says in answer to the defendant's case.
RE JUDICATA - A thing judicially acted upon or decided.
RES ADJUDICATA - Doctrine that an issue or dispute litigated and determined in a case between the opposing parties is deemed permanently decided between these parties.
RESCIND (RECISSION) - To avoid or cancel a contract.
RESPONDENT - A defendant in a proceeding in chancery or admiralty; also, the person who contends against the appeal in a case.
RESTITUTION - In equity, it is the restoration of both parties to their original condition (when practicable), upon the rescission of a contract for fraud or similar cause.
RETROACTIVE (RETROSPECTIVE) - Looking back; effective as of a prior time.
REVERSED - A term used by appellate courts to indicate that the decision of the lower court in the case before it has been set aside.
REVOKE - To recall or cancel.
RIPARIAN (RIGHTS) - The rights of a person owning land containing or bordering on a water course or other body of water, such as lakes and rivers.

S

SALE - A contract whereby the ownership of property is transferred from one person to another for a sum of money or for any consideration.
SANCTION - A penalty or punishment provided as a means of enforcing obedience to a law; also, an authorization.
SATISFACTION - The discharge of an obligation by paying a party what is due to him; or what is awarded to him by the judgment of a court or otherwise.
SCIENTER - Knowingly; also, it is used in pleading to denote the defendant's guilty knowledge.
SCINTILLA - A spark; also the least particle.
SECRET OF STATE - Governmental secret relating to the national defense or the international relations of the United States.
SECURITY - Indemnification; the term is applied to an obligation, such as a mortgage or deed of trust, given by a debtor to insure the payment or performance of his debt, by furnishing the creditor with a resource to be used in case of the debtor's failure to fulfill the principal obligation.
SENTENCE - The judgment formally pronounced by the court or judge upon the defendant after his conviction in a criminal prosecution.
SET-OFF - A claim or demand which one party in an action credits against the claim of the opposing party.
SHALL and MAY - "Shall" is mandatory and "may" is permissive.
SITUS - Location.
SOVEREIGN - A person, body or state in which independent and supreme authority is vested.
STARE DECISIS - To follow decided cases.

STATE - "State" means this State, unless applied to the different parts of the United States. In the latter case, it includes any state, district, commonwealth, territory or insular possession of the United States, including the District of Columbia.

STATEMENT - (a) Oral or written verbal expression or (b) nonverbal conduct of a person intended by him as a substitute for oral or written verbal expression.

STATUTE - An act of the legislature. Includes a treaty.

STATUTE OF LIMITATION - A statute limiting the time to bring an action after the right of action has arisen.

STAY - To hold in abeyance an order of a court.

STIPULATION - Any agreement made by opposing attorneys regulating any matter incidental to the proceedings or trial.

SUBORDINATION (AGREEMENT) - An agreement making one's rights inferior to or of a lower rank than another's.

SUBORNATION - The crime of procuring a person to lie or to make false statements to a court.

SUBPOENA - A writ or order directed to a person, and requiring his attendance at a particular time and place to testify as a witness.

SUBPOENA DUCES TECUM - A subpoena used, not only for the purpose of compelling witnesses to attend in court, but also requiring them to bring with them books or documents which may be in their possession, and which may tend to elucidate the subject matter of the trial.

SUBROGATION - The substituting of one for another as a creditor, the new creditor succeeding to the former's rights.

SUBSIDY - A government grant to assist a private enterprise deemed advantageous to the public.

SUI GENERIS - Of the same kind.

SUIT - Any civil proceeding by a person or persons against another or others in a court of justice by which the plaintiff pursues the remedies afforded him by law.

SUMMONS - A notice to a defendant that an action against him has been commenced and requiring him to appear in court and answer the complaint.

SUPRA - Above; this word occurring by itself in a book refers the reader to a previous part of the book.

SURETY - A person who binds himself for the payment of a sum of money, or for the performance of something else, for another.

SURPLUSAGE - Extraneous or unnecessary matter.

SURVIVORSHIP - A term used when a person becomes entitled to property by reason of his having survived another person who had an interest in the property.

SUSPEND SENTENCE - Hold back a sentence pending good behavior of prisoner.

SYLLABUS - A note prefixed to a report, especially a case, giving a brief statement of the court's ruling on different issues of the case.

T

TALESMAN - Person summoned to fill a panel of jurors.

TENANT - One who holds or possesses lands by any kind of right or title; also, one who has the temporary use and occupation of real property owned by another person (landlord), the duration and terms of his tenancy being usually fixed by an instrument called "a lease."

TENDER - An offer of money; an expression of willingness to perform a contract according to its terms.

TERM - When used with reference to a court, it signifies the period of time during which the court holds a session, usually of several weeks or months duration.

TESTAMENTARY - Pertaining to a will or the administration of a will.
TESTATOR (male)
TESTATRIX (female) - One who makes or has made a testament or will.
TESTIFY (TESTIMONY) - To give evidence under oath as a witness.
TO WIT - That is to say; namely.
TORT - Wrong; injury to the person.
TRANSITORY - Passing from place to place.
TRESPASS - Entry into another's ground, illegally.
TRIAL - The examination of a cause, civil or criminal, before a judge who has jurisdiction over it, according to the laws of the land.
TRIER OF FACT - Includes (a) the jury and (b) the court when the court is trying an issue of fact other than one relating to the admissibility of evidence.
TRUST - A right of property, real or personal, held by one party for the benefit of another.
TRUSTEE - One who lawfully holds property in custody for the benefit of another.

U

UNAVAILABLE AS A WITNESS - The declarant is (1) Exempted or precluded on the ground of privilege from testifying concerning the matter to which his statement is relevant; (2) Disqualified from testifying to the matter; (3) Dead or unable to attend or to testify at the hearing because of then existing physical or mental illness or infirmity; (4) Absent from the hearing and the court is unable to compel his attendance by its process; or (5) Absent from the hearing and the proponent of his statement has exercised reasonable diligence but has been unable to procure his attendance by the court's process.
ULTRA VIRES - Acts beyond the scope and power of a corporation, association, etc.
UNILATERAL - One-sided; obligation upon, or act of one party.
USURY - Unlawful interest on a loan.

V

VACATE - To set aside; to move out.
VARIANCE - A discrepancy or disagreement between two instruments or two aspects of the same case, which by law should be consistent.
VENDEE - A purchaser or buyer.
VENDOR - The person who transfers property by sale, particularly real estate; the term "seller" is used more commonly for one who sells personal property.
VENIREMEN - Persons ordered to appear to serve on a jury or composing a panel of jurors.
VENUE - The place at which an action is tried, generally based on locality or judicial district in which an injury occurred or a material fact happened.
VERDICT - The formal decision or finding of a jury.
VERIFY - To confirm or substantiate by oath.
VEST - To accrue to.
VOID - Having no legal force or binding effect.
VOIR DIRE - Preliminary examination of a witness or a juror to test competence, interest, prejudice, etc.

W

WAIVE - To give up a right.
WAIVER - The intentional or voluntary relinquishment of a known right.
WARRANT (WARRANTY) (v.) - To promise that a certain fact or state of facts, in relation to the subject matter, is, or shall be, as it is represented to be.

WARRANT (n.) - A writ issued by a judge, or other competent authority, addressed to a sheriff, or other officer, requiring him to arrest the person therein named, and bring him before the judge or court to answer or be examined regarding the offense with which he is charged.

WRIT - An order or process issued in the name of the sovereign or in the name of a court or judicial officer, commanding the performance or nonperformance of some act.

WRITING - Handwriting, typewriting, printing, photostating, photographing and every other means of recording upon any tangible thing any form of communication or representation, including letters, words, pictures, sounds, or symbols, or combinations thereof.

WRITINGS AND RECORDINGS - Consists of letters, words, or numbers, or their equivalent, set down by handwriting, typewriting, printing, photostating, photographing, magnetic impulse, mechanical or electronic recording, or other form of data compilation.

Y

YEA AND NAY - Yes and no.

YELLOW DOG CONTRACT - A contract by which employer requires employee to sign an instrument promising as condition that he will not join a union during its continuance, and will be discharged if he does join.

Z

ZONING - The division of a city by legislative regulation into districts and the prescription and application in each district of regulations having to do with structural and architectural designs of buildings and of regulations prescribing use to which buildings within designated districts may be put.

www.ingramcontent.com/pod-product-compliance
Lightning Source LLC
Chambersburg PA
CBHW081818300426
44116CB00014B/2403